Say it

with confidence

Sarah Sutton

The 7 Step Plan

B B C ACTIVE

BBC Active, an imprint of Educational Publishers LLP, part of the
Pearson Education Group
Edinburgh Gate
Harlow
Essex CM20 2JE
England

First published in 2006 by BBC Active

ISBN-10: 0-563-52000-0
ISBN-13: 978-0-563-52000-9

Commissioning Editor: Emma Shackleton
Project Editor: Helena Caldon
Text Designer: Annette Peppis
Cover Designer: Annette Peppis
Production Controller: Man Fai Lau

Printed and bound by Ashford Colour Press Ltd, UK

The Publisher's policy is to use paper manufactured from sustainable forests.

Contents

Acknowledgements

Many of the practical exercises used in this book have been adapted from the BBC business skills courses *Say the Right Thing* and *Confidence Zone*. For further details, please see the bibliography. The contributing experts are fully and gratefully acknowledged for their expertise and for permission to reproduce excerpts from the training guides that accompanied the series. My role has been to distil and interpret their knowledge and expertise for the general reader.

With grateful thanks to: Emma Shackleton, Annette Peppis, Helena Caldon and the team at BBC Active; and to all those who contributed their experiences and stories.

Preface

Confidence n *(1) A consciousness of being sufficient; a feeling of reliance; self-assurance. (2) faith or trust in something or somebody. (3) certainty or strong expectation*

ADAPTED FROM *THE PENGUIN ENGLISH DICTIONARY*

Our wish to connect with other people, and to have our needs recognized and met, begins at the moment that we first draw breath and continues throughout life as we build relationships and learn to listen and communicate with people at home, socially and in the workplace. We all want some consideration and to be appreciated for who we are.

However, just because we have something to say does not automatically mean that we will be heard – or fully understood. A tendency to be too passive, too aggressive, or to be unfocused when speaking, can mean 'missing the moment' to get a point across effectively. Being misunderstood, passed over, excluded or undermined as a result of giving out the wrong signals, not knowing what to say or how to say it, can be frustrating, stressful and a blow to self-esteem.

Having confidence in your ability to raise a sensitive issue, communicate important information, or give a clear instruction is an important life skill, and vital for getting ahead in business. Equally important is the ability to give and receive positive feedback in personal and professional relationships. The ideal way to succeed is to adopt a style that respects the views of others, and to have the skills and the confidence to state your own needs in a clear and focused way.

Say It With Confidence is a practical guide to being assertive and feeling at ease when expressing your needs and opinions. The steps and guidelines in this book are based on successful professional techniques that will help you to understand your current style of communication, to find your voice, to make yourself heard, and to discover how to express your desires and opinions so that they will be listened to and respected – whatever the situation.

You don't speak only with your voice; you communicate with your eyes, your gestures and your body language too. The following chapters will explore what confident communication looks and sounds like; your personal style of behaviour; your self-belief; how you talk to yourself; how to speak up for what you want, and how to say what you mean in an effective manner. Step by step, the book will provide the practical skills you need to help you plan, prepare for and face everyday situations.

Each of the steps has been designed to help you to develop awareness of the impact that you have on other people. Specifically, to see yourself through others' eyes and to provide you with simple but powerful tools to transform the way you think, speak and behave – whether you're on your own, or in company.

If you can develop the ability to say what you mean,

and mean what you say, without fear of being judged, criticized or rejected, you will gain respect from yourself and others, and you will be closer to releasing your true potential in life.

Introduction

Release your potential

'The possibilities are numerous, once we start to act and not react.'

GEORGE BERNARD SHAW

This book is one of a series of titles that looks at the life skills needed to release your potential and become the best you can be – and want to be. *Say It With Confidence* is about finding your voice: being able to express your opinions, share your views, speak up for yourself and, if necessary, assert your rights. Whether you call it confidence or assertiveness, the ability to express yourself directly and reasonably in a non-aggressive way is an essential part of being true to yourself and making the most of your abilities and potential.

For some people, speaking up appears to be easy. They have no qualms about standing their ground, stating their opinion, presenting in public or making sure that their needs are taken into account. Their assertive behaviour shows in their ability to communicate confidently and competently.

For others, there are challenges to face before their voice can be heard. Concerns about what to say, when and how to say it, and how they will be judged, can impede action to such an extent that, in the end, what is said 'comes out all wrong' – or they may say nothing at all.

The majority of people who make it to the top in business are those who have mastered the art of assertive communication – it is at the heart of strong management and helps teams work together effectively. Similarly, at home, being an assertive parent, partner or child (as opposed to being passive or aggressive in approach) means having respect for the opinions of others, rather than taking a one-sided stance. This does not mean backing down, or compromising your own viewpoint, but it does mean making sure that everyone has their say, and feels they have been listened to.

Assertiveness is easiest to maintain if you practise it all the time, rather than adopting a stance for specific occasions. Being clear and focused in what you say, remaining open to the points of view of others, and having the inner confidence to think and behave in a positive manner will have an impact on you as well as on those around you – before you say a word. Confident and calm communication helps to resolve disagreements and ease decision-making in a way that respects the feelings of others, but, at the same time, ensures that there is a mutually beneficial result to all discussions and situations.

If that sounds hard to achieve, read on. Most of us are passive in some situations and defensive or aggressive in others. Finding the mid-point can be a challenge – especially if feelings are running high.

The skills of confident communication need practice and it takes focused effort to change ingrained habits that are undermining your own success. However, the techniques themselves are straightforward, logical and easy to learn, and once you take the plunge to apply them you will find that your communication skills improve immediately.

Whose life is it anyway?

Throughout school and growing up we are encouraged not to be selfish, how to consider the needs of other people, and to think about things from their point of view. These ground rules are about being just, fair and recognizing that we each have an equal role to play. For some, however, it becomes second nature to consider other people's needs *ahead* of their own. Although commendable in some situations, the danger of taking this attitude to extremes is that it can be personally challenging for such people to recognize when their own needs should come first. The adult who is living their life the way that he or she thinks their partner, child, boss or parent wants them to, will find it hard to do it their own way and to discover their own skills and abilities.

Developing the ability to be assertive and self-confident enriches relationships of all kinds, as it puts people on an equal footing and encourages fair exchange of ideas and mutual respect. Taking responsibility for your own thoughts, ideas and actions means that you live your own life – not someone else's.

Releasing potential in the workplace

Many people spend more hours at work than they do at home or with friends and family. Feeling comfortable expressing opinions and having the skills to retain other people's respect and attention is relevant every day – from relating to colleagues, to making a presentation, pitching for business, negotiating an increase in pay or resolving a difference of opinion.

Knowing when and how to speak up can be challenging for many reasons: concern about your position, job security, knowledge and experience, or what people might think. All these factors will lead the individual to decide when and whether to speak or stay silent.

In order to make things happen you need to take action and make yourself heard. This is true whether you are ambitious to progress or you have a problem to resolve.

If someone's actions are having a negative impact on you, you have a right to point out the effects of their behaviour. The important thing is to get your view across calmly, stating your point of view in a balanced way and without losing control of your emotions. To reach a solution that benefits all involved it is also important to understand the other person's point of view – even if you don't agree with it. The keys to success are a combination of focus, firmness, listening and respect for all parties, with the aim of reaching a mutually beneficial solution.

Presenting yourself to others can be nerve-wracking, even in a positive situation (such as making a thank you speech to a group of people or raising an issue at a meeting). So finding the right words to make your point to someone who is being aggressive, negative or bullying can be even more of a challenge.

In just such a predicament, Laura recalls her first job, where she forced herself to resolve a difficult situation because it was undermining her ability to do her job well and was resulting in personal stress.

'When I was in my first job at assistant level, I had a boss who was badly organized and poor at delegating. He would alter a brief at a moment's notice, never allowed enough time to get the job done, didn't keep progress notes and so never remembered what had been said. When things went wrong (as they often did) it became my fault – for 'not listening', for 'misunderstanding', for 'doing the wrong thing', and so on. Instead of taking responsibility for his actions, he became aggressive and turned into a bully. I didn't have the experience to know how to handle the situation and so it became increasingly stressful, to the point that I nearly left the job because of him – his approach was undermining my belief in my ability.

Fortunately, I had a period of time out to review things when I was on holiday. I did some reading on the subject of assertiveness and talked to my boyfriend about the situation. I came to realize that I needed to take responsibility for my response to my boss's behaviour and that I should stand up to him and explain what I needed from him to do my job effectively. Any other decision would have impacted on my whole career.

When I came back to work I was prepared. I managed to contain my emotions and I explained to him that it was unacceptable for him to blame me for the poor planning and delivery of projects, and that his attitude was disrespectful and threatening. I had prepared in advance some recommendations for practical changes that could be made in order to improve communication and work flow. In focusing on these solutions we were able to reach a joint resolution that turned the situation around.

It wasn't long before I decided to stop working for him anyway, but it was a vital lesson for me. It took a lot of courage at the time, and looking back I am proud that I managed to confront the situation effectively. Had I not done so, I can see that my previously passive response might have become a recurring pattern throughout my career.'

Laura's experience is played out in different ways in offices and work scenarios every day. Her boss may have been quite young and inexperienced himself; he didn't know how to manage his team and was a poor communicator. He, too, needed to learn how to be assertive – instead of aggressive. The positive outcomes from his point of view were that his work would have improved as a result of Laura's input and he gained some invaluable feedback regarding the impact of his aggressive attitude and management style. His own potential for success should have increased with that knowledge – if he chose to take it on board.

The positive outcomes for Laura were that she resolved the situation in a considered and mature way; she gained confidence in her ability to manage conflict and saw that she could face difficult situations without losing control of her emotions. By confronting the issue she gained the respect and appreciation of her boss, and, importantly, she retained her self-esteem. In being courageous she had developed her potential to manage other situations in the future.

Assertiveness is not about achieving a personal 'win' or about attacking a person who has upset you. It is about true communication that is constructive and beneficial to all involved. Until you learn to express your true feelings, you won't be able to achieve all you want to.

The assertiveness audit

Take ten minutes now to think of areas in your life that would improve if you became more assertive.

Examples include:

❍ Putting the needs of others before your own

❍ Stating what your needs are

❍ Dealing with authority figures – for example, doctors, lawyers, teachers or parents

❍ Being comfortable making presentations

❍ Managing meetings effectively

❍ Voicing your ideas and opinions

❍ Delegating and following through

❍ Dealing with a difficult person

❍ Voicing disagreement

○ Managing conflict
○ Talking to people you don't know
○ Being looked at or noticed
○ Doing things on your own
○ Trying something new
○ Booking tickets and making reservations
○ Being comfortable using the telephone
○ Complaining about poor service
○ Standing up to your partner or family
○ Telling people what you want – for example, a builder,
hairdresser or estate agent
○ Not wanting to offend
○ Talking about sensitive issues
○ Standing up to a stranger
○ Having personal presence.

Think about the ways in which you would fulfil your potential if you were more assertive – whether at work, in your leisure and social time, or at home and in your relationships.

Which three areas of your life are the most important for you to concentrate on at the moment? Decide on these, and make them your priority for taking action. Keep them in the forefront of your mind as you work through the book.

Now create a list of the same length to highlight areas where you believe that you *are* assertive.

Once you've done this, think: what is it that makes you confident in one situation and not in another?

The following chapters will help you to address these points and help to turn your doubts into reasons for positive action.

Few people, not even life's highest achievers, feel as confident as they would like to be in every situation, and, for many, an inability to stay calm under pressure can be a real challenge. The difference between appearing confident and assured, or passive, manipulative or aggressive, will come across to others, and the results of changing your approach can be dramatic. At work, it may mean the difference between winning and losing a business opportunity or a pay rise; as a manager or parent it can mean commanding respect or losing control; socially, it is the contrast between feeling able to speak to someone you find attractive or interesting, or being inhibited by the fear and embarrassment of becoming tongue-tied. There are as many scenarios as there are people and situations.

Why should someone who feels confident expressing their opinions as a parent feel less able to speak up at work? Why does someone who performs well in the workplace feel less able to be themselves in a social situation? Why would a student who has no problem expressing himself on paper have weak presentation skills?

The answer lies not in what we know, but in what we believe – about ourselves.

Confidence is expressed through gestures, style of speech, a way of dressing, or a confident stance – but it begins in the mind. It is about self-belief and having a sense of competence.

The purpose of this book is to help you to develop practical communication skills and positive belief in your ability to be assertive in approach. If you understand your personal style and how you come across to other people when you speak, it will help you to choose an appropriate tone of voice, style of language and gestures. In a very short space of time it will be possible to adjust your style according to your circumstances, and you will have developed a more positive sense of yourself as an effective communicator.

If you feel comfortable with who you are, and know you can rely on yourself to cope with any scenario without feeling rattled, put upon or victimized, then you have the ability to achieve anything you put your mind to. All you need to do to begin to express yourself appropriately and assertively is learn a few practical techniques.

Acting confident

To get a sense of how you react when you are assertive, think of a moment when you were feeling at ease, comfortable, relaxed and able to talk and when you got your point across freely without fear of conflict, criticism or being challenged.

Really focus on the event in your mind and pay attention to your senses:

○ How do you *look* when you are expressing yourself confidently?
○ How do you *sound?*
○ How do you *feel?*

The chances are that you will become more relaxed as you hold this image, as you remember your positive feelings and associations. In an instant, you have transformed your state into something more positive and confident by using your senses to tune into your memory and to remember how you felt at a moment in time.

A confident person:
○ *looks* comfortable, engaged, interested
○ *sounds* assertive, relaxed, energized
○ *feels* uplifted, positive, outward-facing, connected

The results of behaving confidently are self-generating. People who have a confident outlook attract and encourage the people around them. The person who can project a positive presence and draw in positive thoughts and feelings will communicate confidence to others before they have uttered a single word.

Assertiveness does not always guarantee the outcome you want – but it does mean that you will be listened to, and that everyone has a fair say.

Anyone can be assertive, although it may take practice to perfect the technique. If you tend naturally to be quite quiet, then being assertive may feel uncomfortable to begin with. You may feel your voice is too loud, that you are being too pushy or dislike the direct attention. (If this sounds like you, then see the 'over the top' exercise on p. 88 to help you to find your voice.)

Likewise, if you are more likely to take a challenging stance when you are under pressure, then you may find that an assertive approach will feel like compromise or weakness until you start to get results. (If this sounds like you, practising putting yourself in another's shoes before speaking will give space to gain some perspective.)

The saying goes that 'the definition of insanity is to keep doing what you're doing but to expect a *different* result'. If you have reached a point where you would like a different result, you will need to accept that you have to experience a brief period of learning and discomfort while you change your current approach or behaviour.

If you are able to develop your assertiveness skills, you will automatically grow in confidence and feel more comfortable in every social, formal and business situation. Confidence-building techniques and the ability to communicate effectively are not just empty skills – they will bring positive rewards that can transform all areas of your life.

Take the first step

Confidence and assertiveness are cornerstones of contentment and achievement in life. Whether your ambition is to succeed in business, to make a fortune, to gain a place in your local football team, to be acknowledged as a talented artist, or to be a better parent, your ability to succeed will be enhanced if you can recognize when you are acting in a way that is not in your best interests.

Passive, manipulative, bullying and aggressive behaviours may seem to have nothing in common – but at their heart is a fearful, 'me-centred' approach that will ultimately hold you back from gaining support, respect and recognition when you most need it.

Look back at the assertiveness audit you completed on p. 18 and consider how your life could be improved if you were able to use an assertive approach to reach your current goals. Achieving the change will motivate you to aim higher next time, because your previous obstacles will no longer be there.

The first step is to know who you are and to understand your current personal style. The next chapter will help you to take stock of how you think and how you behave, and where the problems might lie, before moving on to the practical guidelines for change and transformation.

① Who are you?
Understanding your personal style

'I was always looking outside myself for strength and confidence, but it comes from within. It is there all the time.'

ANNA FREUD, AUSTRIAN PSYCHOANALYST AND PSYCHOLOGIST (1895–1982)

This chapter looks at the roots of personal confidence; the power of personal impact; the possible gap between your self-image and how you believe you are perceived; and the reality of how you come across to others. The contrasts between personal myth and practical reality can be quite dramatic.

Communicating with confidence

At the root of confident behaviour and communication is the ability to be assertive. The concept of assertiveness is sometimes wrongly confused with aggressiveness or pushiness, but it is neither of those. Assertiveness is not about being domineering; it is about being able to communicate with respect – respect for your own opinions as well as those of others. It does not mean pushing your viewpoint at the expense of other people's, and nor does it mean that a compromise is inevitable. In order to communicate effectively and honestly, assertive behaviour means being positive, creative, clear and fair. Importantly, it is also about taking responsibility for your own feelings and opinions. If you want someone to understand your point of view, you need to let them know what it is.

Confident and assertive behaviour is self-generating and encourages similar behaviour in other people. It looks, sounds and feels comfortable and empowering. Lack of confidence and a sense of powerlessness, on the other hand, will lead to symptoms of anxiety. Anxiety triggers a mixture of responses. Some people will cope by reacting *aggressively* to their situation (the 'fight' response), while others will cope by reacting *passively* (the 'flight' response); it depends on personality.

Do you recognize any of the following characteristics as your own, either when in a new or uncomfortable situation, or when you feel you have been denied your say?

Passive behaviour	**Aggressive behaviour**
Avoiding eye contact	Glaring/staring
Quiet, strained voice	Loud voice
Sentences not finished	Lots of interruptions
Flushed face	Flushed face
Nervous hand movements	Finger wagging
Backing away physically from someone	Moving towards the other person
Apologizing frequently	Blaming
Frequent nodding in agreement	Frowning/head shaking
Agreeing without questioning	Stating opinions as facts

The passive response

The long-term consequences of suppressing your personality and opinions through constant passive behaviour can be dramatic. Panic attacks, depression, fearfulness, an inability to accept criticism, a reluctance to complain or state your own opinion: all of these responses, and others, will chip away at your self-esteem as day after day and week after week you deny your true self and avoid confrontation or risk.

People who are mainly passive can come across as manipulative on occasion, as they may try to exert their influence by blocking an action rather than by disagreeing or stating their differing point of view.

Common passive responses include:
❍ Saying 'yes' when you want to say 'no'.
❍ Complying rather than risk a disagreement.
❍ Agreeing to something that is to your disadvantage rather than chance disapproval.
❍ Smiling and being outwardly pleasant when your true feelings are the opposite.

The aggressive response

Likewise, adopting a perpetual aggressive, defensive, or complaining response can leave you socially isolated, may threaten your personal health (by boosting blood pressure), as well as being stressful and unpleasant for those on the receiving end of your unhappiness.

Common aggressive responses include:
○ Saying 'no' on principle, even when it is to your own disadvantage.
○ Challenging and undermining rather than discussing or seeking a compromise.
○ Criticizing the person rather than the action.
○ Using body language to intimidate others or to show that you are unhappy.

Behaviour that is passive or defensive is used as a defence strategy, stemming from an expectation that you will not be heard. Most people adopt a mix of both passive and aggressive responses, sometimes displaying both at the same time.

What's your style?

To help you to assess how well you know yourself, take some time to complete the following questionnaire.

There are no right or wrong answers, and no one need see the results but you. The more honest you can be with yourself, and the more self-aware you are, the more easily you should learn to take a more positive or assertive stance.

Do you react passively, aggressively or assertively in the following situations?
○ When being criticized – justly
○ When being criticized – unjustly
○ When wanting to say 'no'
○ When feeling rejected or excluded

○ When not consulted about a decision that affects you directly

○ When wanting to complain

○ When someone disagrees with you

○ When interrupted

○ When wanting to criticize someone

○ When feeling low in confidence or self-esteem

○ When feeling tired or under stress

○ When something does not turn out as planned

○ When feeling under threat

○ When you feel embarrassed

Look at the balance between your passive, aggressive and assertive responses. Has one trait shown up as more dominant that the rest?

Take a closer look at your trigger points and your reactions when confidence is at a low ebb. What are the traits you'd like to change?

When do you tend to react passively?

_____

_____

How do you behave when you do?

_____

_____

When do you tend to react aggressively or defensively?

_____

_____

_____

How do you behave when you do?

_____

_____

When do you tend to react assertively?

_____

_____

How do you behave when you do?

_____

_____

What kinds of thoughts trigger your reactions?

_____

_____

What are the personal costs or benefits to you of these reactions?

_____

_____

What would you like to change about your reactions?

_____

_____

These results are your focal points for personal action and change. Keep them to hand as you read this book.

Starting young

Many of the ways that we choose to communicate are rooted in behaviours that we learnt in childhood. Some of those behaviours remain appropriate as we grow older, and others should be left behind. For example, enjoying praise for a job well done shows positive acceptance of your abilities and achievement, whereas an inability to accept constructive criticism points to a personal insecurity that is self-limiting.

Childhood labels are an inevitable part of life:

At home: A child may be labelled as good, bad, pretty, clever, the oldest, the youngest, just like his/her mother/ father, sickly, accident-prone, and so on, and can often be compared with other siblings.

At school: Children are labelled as good at some subjects, bad at others, 'always' in trouble, a bad influence, a good example, not as clever as a brother/sister, sporty, bright, dyslexic, and so on.

In the playground: Children can be very harsh. A child who stands out in some way because of the way they look, dress, are praised or told off, will attract nicknames. Some of these names will be affectionate; others have the potential to scar the child for life.

Adults, like children, will tend to seek out good news first, but have a tendency to give undue credence to the bad. There is a part of your memory that will continue to remember your childhood labels and you may find that some of those labels still dominate your feelings about yourself and your levels of ability. This is especially true in situations where we feel we have under-performed or have let ourselves down. Labels that stick and that are taken to heart (and mind) have a greater chance of becoming a self-fulfilling prophecy. (See Chapter 2 for information on how our thoughts and words reinforce our self-image, actions and self-belief.)

Understanding what kinds of labels we give ourselves can be a very useful way of identifying the obstacles that are preventing us from fulfilling our true potential, as well as highlighting our personal strengths and recognizing how we are viewed by others. Once we understand how we are holding ourselves back, we can do something about changing this situation, and re-framing the ways in which we think about ourselves.

The labelling exercise

Take approximately five minutes in total to list five words that describe you best in each of the following categories:

Your own view of yourself:

_____

_____

The view of a superior at work, or another authority figure:

_____

_____

The view of a relative or partner:

_____

_____

Don't pause to deliberate for too long, as your first thoughts will be best. When you have filled all the spaces, read through each list and judge whether your words, phrases or traits are positive or negative in each instance. Place a plus or minus sign next to each word as relevant.

Take time to reflect:

○ Overall, did you have more positives or negatives?
○ Did the negatives cluster more strongly in one section than in the others?
○ When you listed a negative point, did you consciously counter it by thinking of a positive point, or did one negative thought lead to another?

Now revisit the exercise and choose to replace all the negative traits with positive ones. Choose five words that you think describe you most accurately, and write them down. This is to remind you that it is positive words that drive us forward to success. (See Chapter 2 for guidance on positive thinking and Chapter 3 for more about personal motivation.)

This exercise will help you to see where your own labels originated:

○ Did they come from you, or from someone else?
○ Do they reflect how you think of yourself all the time? Or only in certain moments?
○ Who are you trying to please? Yourself or someone else?
○ Which voices do you listen to the most? Your own? Or others'?

As adults in a modern world we need to be able to choose our own labels, to make sure they are an accurate reflection of our positive traits and abilities. Adult behaviour means learning to take constructive criticism on board rather than responding to it defensively; it means taking responsibility for positive achievements as well as errors of judgement; and learning to adapt our behaviour in line with the needs of a situation, if necessary. (Adaptability is not the same as unquestioning compliance, as we shall see.) Once you know which styles of behaviour you normally favour, you will be able to decide where your strengths lie and which areas you need to improve, so that you will be able to move forward more quickly.

Making an impact

At the root of confident behaviour is the willingness to accept yourself as you are; to accept or change those aspects that you would rather not have; and to make the most of your attributes and skills. Does the simple phrase, 'Be yourself!' give you a sense of relief, or does it send you into a spiral of uncertainty? If the latter is true, the chances are that you will find it hard to express yourself on occasion; that you may be unduly concerned about what others think; or fearful of rejection if 'being you' doesn't fit the norm. There are no fixed reasons as to why one person will behave confidently and another will not. Your concerns may have their roots in childhood behaviour, in 'wrong thinking' about your abilities, or may be related to a simpler concern about a lack of basic skills and techniques.

There are several practical exercises in this section that will help you to re-think your beliefs about yourself, and help you to turn any doubts and fears into opportunities for living more confidently.

Ask yourself:

○ Are you aware of the impact that you have on other people, or are you more aware of the impact they have on you?

○ Do you see yourself as others see you, or is there a perception gap?

Developing confidence in your ability to make a positive impact is your first step towards making things happen in the way that you would like them to.

If you want to take a serious look at your own style of communication, you may like to arrange for someone to watch or even film you in action – whilst in discussion, making a presentation or when actively listening – so you can see for yourself how you come across in conversation or in public. For those without access to a video or camera phone, however, the following technique will help you to get to the heart of who you really think you are, and how that can affect the impact you have on those around you.

The following exercise is recommended by psychologist Ros Taylor, who uses it as a first step in getting to know her clients and gaining an insight into how they see themselves.

The self-portrait

Give yourself time to focus on this exercise uninterrupted. All you will need is a blank sheet of A4 paper, something to draw with and some time.

You are going sketch a self-portrait. This could take as few as two minutes, or it may take as many as ten. Use as much or as little of the paper as you choose to sketch a drawing of how you see yourself. The exercise is not about your drawing ability or creating a work of art; it is to encourage you to express on paper your thoughts about yourself, your appearance and how you are seen by others.

Assessment

If you think you will find it hard to assess your picture with any clarity, consider encouraging someone you trust to try the same exercise and then swap pictures. By looking at each other's pictures and sharing your thoughts, you are more likely to gain an understanding about yourself, your motivation and your confidence levels.

Which part of yourself did you choose to draw? Head only? Head and torso? Whole body?

A whole picture that is drawn in proportion and in a positive way will usually be a sign of self-esteem and being comfortable with personal appearance. Any areas that are left out or distorted are likely to send their own message. For example:

❍ If you drew the head only, consider why you chose to exclude the body and what you were trying to portray.

❍ If you drew a body as well, is it in proportion to the size of your head? If not, why do you think that is?

❍ Which part of your body dominates the picture? Is there a reason for that?

How you draw each element of the head and body will usually give you some insight into how you regard yourself and the impact you think you make on those around you.

Is there anything included in the background of the picture – and if so, what?
Have you added other aspects of your environment to your picture? For example: other people, children, aspects of your work or responsibilities, pets, words or thoughts, something to do with home or holidays. Are they adding positively or negatively to your picture? Does this tell you anything useful about your approach and your situation?

Philip had been overlooked for promotion several times. He was well-liked by his colleagues and respected for his knowledge, but he had an apologetic style of speech and had trouble winning people over with his ideas in meetings. Philip lacked assertiveness skills.

He was confident in his ability, but less happy with his looks. He drew a self-portrait and filled the page with a strong picture of himself with a large, rectangular-shaped head and an exaggeratedly square jaw, then doodled the addition of a computer and screen beside him. In reviewing his efforts he was shocked to see that his face was very tight in expression and the computer screen echoed the shape of his face! In less than two minutes he had drawn a picture that summed up the fact that his identity was very strongly linked with his work. It also helped him to realize that his self-consciousness made him dislike being the centre of attention and that this was an obstacle to his making more progress at work.

The clear lines of the picture and the bold use of the whole page were positive signs that he was not low in self-esteem, so he concluded that he just needed to work on his self-image a little more and to develop some practical communication skills.

How much of the page was used? Was the drawing large or small?
A small self-portrait that doesn't take up much of the available room on the page suggests a tendency towards passive behaviour, and also low levels of self-confidence. A large self-portrait suggests more confident behaviour, depending upon the other elements included.

Are the lines used bold or weak?
A picture drawn with weak lines, tentative strokes and lack of definition will suggest low self-esteem and a lack of certainty about self-image.

A picture drawn with bold lines and strokes suggests a strong sense of self and less likelihood of problems with self-esteem.

Did you draw yourself in a positive way, or is the picture detracting from you?
Consider whether you have enhanced your features in a way that is appealing (for example, full lips, good figure, attractive eyes) or whether you have drawn an image that is in some way negative (for example, a frowning face, exaggeratedly negative features).

If you have drawn a picture of yourself as appealing, consider whether you worry that people respond to your looks rather than to your personality.

An exaggeratedly negative picture may suggest that concern about your appearance influences your ability to be assertive or confident.

What is the mood of the picture?
Have you drawn yourself as happy or sad? Depressed or joyful? Confident or lacking in confidence? Intense or open? All these factors will add to the overall sense of whether you view yourself in a positive or negative light. Consider whether the picture is showing your current mood, a mood you would like to be in, or one you would like to avoid.

How does your sense of confidence relate to your self-image?
Consider whether the picture is a true representation of how you feel inside, or whether you have drawn the face you feel you ought to be showing to the world. Is it positive or negative? Is it a picture of you now, as you'd like to be, or as you used to be?

A positive picture of the present or future is an encouraging vision of self-esteem and confidence. Sometimes, however, the roles we adopt are so ingrained that we no longer know where the role stops and the person starts. It is possible to find we are holding on to a negative and outdated image because our thoughts do not always keep pace with progress and reality.

Would close friends or family see you the way that you see yourself? (If you're unsure, and can trust them to be constructive in their response, try showing them your drawing and ask them their opinions.)

Julian had excelled academically throughout his school and university years and so was used to succeeding and was highly ambitious. His portrait was large, bold, smiling, handsome and showed him holding the trophy he won in a sailing competition during his final year.

He was dismissive of the portrait exercise and couldn't see any benefit to it at all, until his sister pointed out that he was illustrating a very idealised image of himself that was in contrast to how he felt in his current job. The image showed his achievements, whereas at work he was frustrated at his slow progress up the corporate ladder and was very sensitive to criticism. His application for an internal promotion had recently been turned down.

Julian was constantly belittling his less well-qualified colleagues behind their backs and felt irritated and frustrated that his ideas weren't being listened to by senior management. Used to receiving accolades, he did not handle criticism (or what he perceived as failure) well, and didn't see his lack of practical experience as a hurdle to progress. In an honest discussion with his sister, he gradually came to see that the rejection he was experiencing was not personal, and that his attitude towards his colleagues could be perceived as arrogant or belligerent. As a result of this, he realized that he had to show an appreciation of the needs of the team and the department, rather than just himself, in order to be taken seriously at work.

Julian's strong self-confidence meant that he had no qualms about approaching his manager to voice his disappointment and to ask about his long-term prospects. However, armed with a new, increased awareness of how his approach could be misinterpreted, Julian focused first on asking his manager about his aims for the team and the department before asking for an increased opportunity to gain practical experience with a view to aiming for fast-track promotion.

His boss noticed his calmer and more mature approach and respected his ambition, so he agreed to reconsider Julian's application alongside those of others in the department.

You may find it useful to repeat this portrait exercise from time to time in order to see how and whether your self-perception and priorities have changed.

Overcoming fear and managing uncertainty

Having taken a good hard look at your self-image, and any signs of a 'perception gap', the next step is to look at your personal values and sense of motivation.

A major factor in building confidence and assertiveness techniques is developing trust in your own reactions under pressure, and learning that you can survive and manage your anxiety. Easy to say, and less easy to do, you may say! However, it may help you to know that the majority of business people, inventors, explorers and other high achievers who are classed as successful in life, will say that they have learned to take action in spite of their fears, and often before they have all of the facts and knowledge that they need.

The following exercise is a very simple way to get to the heart of your value system: what you see as important in life, and what you would avoid at all costs. Armed with an awareness of your personal 'comfort zone' you will then be able to choose to look at future situations from a different perspective, and to see the positive value in alternative styles of behaviour, depending on circumstances.

Animal instincts

Before reading any further, look at the images of the four animals below, and follow the directions on the following page.

There are no right or wrong answers, and this is not a quiz, so please try to be as honest with yourself as you can be.

1   Choose the animal whose associated qualities you like the most, and write down which of the attributes you admire.

_____

_____

_____

_____

2   Choose your next favourite animal and, again, write down which qualities associated with it you like the most.

_____

_____

_____

_____

3   Make a third choice and, again, write down which of the animal's characteristics you appreciate the most.

_____

_____

_____

_____

4   Look at the animal that is left, and write down what you *dislike* about it, and anything you *fear* about it.

_____

_____

This simple exercise is designed to provide you with insights into your personal values, beliefs, fears and the way that you think.

○ Look first at any similar or repeated words – especially those used to describe the first three pictures that you have chosen. These describe the personal values and characteristics that you consider to be important in life.
○ Look also at any emotional words, because they are an indication of personal passions and enthusiasms.
○ Finally, look at the adjectives you have used to describe animal number 4 – the creature you liked the least. These words will be characteristics that you disapprove of or dislike and they will relate to areas of your life that you fear or that you wish to avoid.
○ Review the negative characteristics. Can you see occasions when these would be positive traits? If you can't, are there other traits associated with the fourth animal that you may lack and that would complement your core values?

Each animal will represent different characteristics to different people. The following summaries show the different values and characteristics chosen by a cross-section of people and will help you to interpret your own results in a meaningful way.

Mary (35)

A part-time information officer and working mother

Dolphin: elegant, beautiful, intelligent, clean
Eagle: powerful, majestic, soaring, beautiful
Squirrel: survivor, entertaining, cute, tidy

Bear: lumbering, bad-tempered, aggressive

The values that Mary associated with the dolphin were order and control; she was attracted to the power and freedom of the eagle and associated the squirrel with lightheartedness and a survival instinct.

Mary was a highly anxious person who found coping with new people and situations extremely difficult. She was married to a man whose values were in many ways opposite to her own. Her repeated words were related to freedom, beauty and order, and showed her how much she craved a new start in life. She was shocked to realize that she associated the negative values of the bear with some of her husband's characteristics – but could also see that other qualities associated with the bear – such as strength, power and determination – could be of value in helping her to communicate with her husband, and to decide on a plan of action for the future.

Zak (23)

Internet entrepreneur

Eagle: Amazing, independent, ruthless, successful, razor-sharp
Bear: A fighter, powerful, dominating, moves easily

Squirrel: Cute, funny, pretty, fast, uncontrollable

*Dolphin: Wet, slimy, whining, new age, goes with the flow,
            vulnerable*

*Zak was a young man with a mission. He wanted to be a
millionaire by the time he was 30. His problem was that he had
failed to win over potential clients and lacked confidence in his
presentation and marketing skills; instead he came across as
'edgy' and impulsive and masked his youthful insecurity with
humour.*

*Zak was not surprised to be told that his repeated phrases
were to do with success, power and ruthlessness, because these
were traits he admired. It took him longer to accept that the traits
he associated with the dolphin could also be turned into positives
that he could benefit from.*

*In his hunger to stand out from the crowd and to blaze a
new trail, Zak had forgotten that he needed to be in tune with
people and to pay attention to their needs too. His business
presentations needed to focus less on his own vision and progress
and more on the needs and benefits of his clients and partners.*

Christa (29)

Call-centre manager

Bear: Powerful, totem, protector, warm, cuddly, strong
Eagle: Glorious, rare, king of birds, majestic
Dolphin: Intelligent, intuitive, mystical, communicative,
             ancient wisdom

Squirrel: Scavenging, rodent, sharp claws, destructive,
vulnerable

Christa chose words that were connected with the themes of intuition, idealism, mysticism and protection. Currently working in the telecoms industry and running a successful team, Christa admitted that she would love to be in a relationship and to have children. She had a fantasy of being whisked away from her role and responsibilities and to be protected and looked after. She had a passion for mythology and ancient legends and spent many weekends hillwalking and painting ancient sites. The traits she admired were not, on their own, helping her to feel grounded.

Christa's parents divorced when she was ten years old and, in spite of her sensitive nature, she found it difficult to get close to people or to build relationships. She automatically expected rejection – and that was being portrayed in her tone of voice and her body language towards men. The negative aspects of the squirrel represented her fear of being on her own, and her defence mechanisms.

Christa used the exercise to focus on her 'squirrel' traits. She replaced the negative qualities of the squirrel with other associations – such as its reputation as a chatterer and communicator; its attractive looks and glossy fur, which make people want to enjoy looking at it; its ability to plan ahead and survive during the winter months and to stand up determinedly against creatures larger than itself.

No matter how confident you are in most areas of life, there will be certain traits that, in vulnerable moments, undermine confidence and the possibility of success. Using a simple device like the 'animal instincts' exercise to get an immediate impression of your frame of mind and your responses, you can consciously focus on making the most of your positive traits, and turning negative traits into opportunities for developing a broader range of skills.

Start where you are

The gap between acting with or without confidence is much smaller than you might think. Both states of mind are the result of training and personal habit. The keys to personal transformation are developing self-belief and the language skills to communicate what you really want and mean in a natural, calm, and assertive way. En route you will be retraining your brain to think positive thoughts so that your senses transmit positive messages to your brain, and so that you look outwards instead of inwards at times of nervousness and anxiety.

The exercises in this book will help you to focus on developing the skills that you already have and to recognize positive traits that you would like to enhance. It will also encourage you to stretch your personal boundaries so that you unleash new abilities you didn't know you had. You will be able to start using the techniques immediately, and you will reap the benefits straight away. With focus and practice you will transform unconfident habits into confident ones, permanently.

First, you need to 'start where you are' in order to take stock of your current skills – and to decide your goals. How do you come across to the people in your life? In what circumstances do you feel you lack confidence? Which personal characteristics need some attention? How do you want things to change? In focusing on these issues and making clear decisions about how, when and what you want to change, you are taking an important step towards personal transformation.

Release your potential – step 1: Know yourself

Appreciate your strengths, know your weaknesses and accept who you are

The ideas and exercises in the introduction and in Chapter 1 are deliberately introspective because before you can act with confidence you need to understand your strengths and weaknesses. Reconciling yourself to who you are is an important step that will help you to understand your actions and reactions.

❍ The self-portrait exercise on p. 36 is a simple but powerful way of revealing your true nature and beliefs. Keep all your drawings over time because you will begin to see yourself differently as you develop confident communication skills. The contrast between early and later drawings will tell its own story.

Your early influences will have had an important impact on the development of your character and the personal impact you in turn have on others. You will often find that the root of your actions and reactions stems from early childhood labelling that you have carried with you into adult life.

❍ Use the exercise on p. 33 to look at the way you label yourself and, if necessary, make a conscious commitment to exchange any negative labels for positive ones.

Your core values are an important aspect of your personality; the stronger and more capable you feel, the more confident you will appear to others.

○ Use the exercise on p. 43 to take stock of your ruling values. Is there a difference between what you believe and what you say? Would your style of communication become more assertive if you expanded your comfort zone to take on some of the positive aspects of traits you are uncomfortable with?

In order to chart your progress and to capture your thoughts and feelings as you increase in confidence, you may find it valuable to begin a journal. It will give you a written account of what drives and motivates you – and will give you honest evidence of your progress, challenges and your moments of success.

Now you have some understanding of the impact of your past and the true nature of the problem you want to solve, the next step is to tackle the driving force behind all our actions. To improve confidence and self-belief, we need to look at the way we think.

② **Think positive**
How to develop self-belief

'Carefully watch your thoughts *for they become your* words.
Manage and watch your words *for they will become your* actions.
Consider and judge your actions *for they have become your* habits.
Acknowledge and watch your habits *for they shall become your* values.
Understand your values *for they become your* destiny.'

MAHATMA GANDHI

Before we begin to *say* things with confidence we need first to begin to *think* them with confidence. What other people say to you will always have an impact, but it's what you say to yourself that really counts. There is a direct connection between developing sound ways of thinking and our levels of self-esteem. The thoughts that you plant today are the seeds of your future actions; they are both a product of, and an instruction to, the brain.

This chapter asks about the messages that you send to your brain when you think. What do you say when you talk to yourself? Is your inner voice encouraging or berating you? Do you gear yourself up to win and take set-backs on the chin, or do you inadvertently undermine your own confidence levels and so live down to, rather than up to, your own expectations? Sometimes a change in perspective is needed in order to see what is going on and to view the events in a different light. Page 71 introduces four steps that can help you to change your perception of reality and decide what action or actions you need to take in order to change your approach in a constructive and positive way.

History, commerce and our daily newspapers are full of examples of people who have triumphed over adversity or who have made it to the top against high odds. The main difference between those people and any one of us is the ability to think – and then act – in an assertive and confident manner. Everything you have ever done began as a thought, and the more you repeat and reinforce your thoughts the more likely they are to turn into deeply-held beliefs.

Mind how you think

At the root of unconfident, passive or aggressive behaviour is a pattern of faulty thinking. Faulty thinking triggers the negative voice that kicks in at inappropriate moments to doubt you and tell you that you are going to fail. It brings with it a sense of powerlessness and anxiety, which is why it tends to trigger the passive or aggressive behaviours listed on p. 27.

Facing up to your fears and dislikes is vital, because you can then take steps to manage and cope with the uncomfortable feelings of anxiety that are triggered at times when we feel at a disadvantage or out of control. There is no point in saying to yourself 'I have no problem giving presentations' if your inner voice is saying 'I'm dreading it', because your brain will know you are lying, and you won't be able to manage your nerves on the day.

A lack of confidence or an inability to express yourself assertively shows up in phrases such as:

'I can't because...'
'I'm not good enough.'
'I'll make a fool of myself.'
'I'll never be able to...'
'I'm hopeless at this.'
'I'm...'

(You can fill in your own variations on the theme.)

How often do you use such phrases? On an occasional, daily, or hourly basis? Is it your natural instinct to be negative rather than positive? If the answer to the second question is 'yes', then try using the following phrases to help you to adjust your perspective and to make sure your inner voice sees your glass as half-full, not half-empty.

'I can because...'
'I need to because...'
'I'm good enough to...'
'I'd like to learn something new.'
'I'd like to improve my skills.'
'I will improve with practice.'
'My opinion is valid.'

If you challenge negative thinking from the outset you can turn unhelpful thoughts into positive alternatives straight away. Modifying your thinking in this way changes not only your frame of mind, but over time it will impact on your habits and actions and have a positive effect on the health, functioning and chemistry of your body as well.

Psychologists have found that it takes an average of 21 days before an old habit can be unlearned and turned into a new behaviour. It then takes two to three months for that new behaviour to become entrenched as a new habit.

The need for approval

At the heart of much of our behaviour is the desire or need for approval from others, and an expectation of reward if we get things right (or punishment if we get things wrong). The threat of being branded with an extreme label such as 'winner' or 'loser', 'success' or 'failure', can lead many people to think themselves out of taking an action in the first place.

Examine the following scenarios and think about what your reactions to them would be. Try to be as honest as possible in your answers and, as you respond, consider whether you are influenced mainly by your own needs, by the needs of others, or by an awareness of the approval or disapproval of those around you.

1   You are in the middle of doing something when the doorbell rings. You open the door to find a young man who asks you who your electricity supplier is and how much you pay each month.

You would:

a   Listen to him politely because it would be rude to interrupt and ask him to stop; possibly invite him in, and consider signing the paperwork. After all, he is only doing his job.

b   Tell him to push off and to stop wasting your time, and shut the door in his face.

c   Say, 'Let me stop you there', and explain that it is not a convenient time and that on principle you will not buy from doorstep sellers. If he would like to leave some literature you may consider following up direct with the company, but you will not be signing anything today.

2   A married friend makes an unexpected pass at you.
You would:

a   Go with the flow; after all, it's him/her who is taking the initiative, so it is not your fault, and you don't want him/her to think you're a spoil-sport.

b   Become angry, pass judgement and threaten to tell his/her partner that he/she is playing away.

c   Ask him/her to stop, explain that his/her action is unexpected, and that you don't want to do anything that either of you would regret later.

3   You are in a group discussion at a social gathering
where it becomes clear that the majority of people hold
a view about a moral issue that is radically different to
your own.

You would:

a   Stay silent. You're a guest in someone's house and
this is not the moment to start raising personal or political
views.

b   Become defensive and personal, using body language
to emphasize your challenge and the fact that you're ready
to take on the group as a whole.

c   State clearly that there is another side to the argument
and ask them to consider your point of view, which differs
from that of the majority present.

4   You have advertised some furniture in the local paper
and a young couple come to view the items. They make an
offer at a level considerably below the asking price, saying
that they have only recently got married and are setting up
their first home together.

You would:

a   Agree to their price. You don't like haggling and they
seem like a nice couple. After all, it would cost money to
advertise again and you don't really want lots of people
coming through your home.

b   Tell them that they are wasting your time and you
don't give handouts. It's your price or no sale.

c   Say that the price is lower than you would be willing
to go, but you wish them well and could knock off a few

pounds as a goodwill gesture for the convenience of them taking the goods straight away.

5   You have eaten a pleasant meal in a restaurant, but when the bill comes it has not been itemized. You add up the total roughly in your head and suspect you may have been over-charged.
    You would:

a   Say nothing and pay the bill. It was tasty food and didn't cost much anyway.

b   Angrily demand a full breakdown of the bill and imply that the owners are pulling a fast one.

c   Call the waiter politely, explain that you would prefer to have an itemized bill and ask calmly whether the bill could be revised to list each of the items ordered.

6   It is the end of year review at work and you find out accidentally that a colleague at the same level as you has had a larger pay rise.
    You would:

a   Say nothing as you're not meant to know, but seethe inwardly with resentment towards your bosses and your colleague.

b   Storm into your boss's office and challenge him/her with the information, demanding that you receive the same level of remuneration as your colleague.

c   Take stock of your role and that of your colleague to see whether there are any obvious differences in experience or levels of responsibility. Then arrange a time to speak to your boss (or HR manager) to discuss your future prospects and to ask for an explanation of existing pay-scales and what might lead one person to have greater rewards than another.

7   You are the sole representative of your company at an important client meeting. Your client is referring to a recent development in company business as if you already know what it is, but you haven't a clue what is being talked about.

You would:

a   Say nothing and bluff. You assume it is your error and that you should have found out about this in advance. Your colleagues at the office will know what your client is talking about and you don't want to look a fool.

b   You ask for an explanation, saying you don't know what he's referring to and blame your colleagues for not having briefed you properly.

c   You ask your client whether he would mind giving you brief background details as you are not familiar with the business he is referring to.

The 'a's are passive responses; the 'b's are aggressive responses and the 'c's are assertive responses. Analyzing your choices will show you your predominant way of thinking or of behaving.

Passive thoughts and responses are more likely to lead to inaction than action. They are generally non-confrontational; involve suppressing personal emotions and preferences; tend to put the needs of others ahead of one's own; show a tendency to want to get along with others and to be liked; and reveal a fear of rejection or judgement.

Aggressive thoughts and responses are more likely to lead to impulsive actions and belligerence. Tone of voice and body language are likely to alienate, dominate and intimidate. An aggressive person has an expectation that they will be treated unfairly if they don't speak up for themselves and they believe that approval should be courted by showing strength of conviction and character, rather than apparent weakness.

Assertive listening, thinking and behaviour are action-orientated. Assertiveness requires a balanced and reasoned approach and focuses on fair outcomes. People who adopt this approach are usually comfortable with themselves, honest about how they feel and how a situation is affecting them; and straightforward in approach. They are comfortable defending a position and don't take disagreement as a sign of personal conflict or rejection.

Rules for life

Many people think of themselves mainly in terms of their roles and responsibilities: wife, husband, parent, partner, plumber, cleaner, managing director, and so on, but you are first and foremost an individual with personal needs, goals and responsibilities. Being assertive can be a challenge if you can't tell where your role stops and your rights as a person begin. The following 'rules for life' are a useful reminder that we are human beings first and our adopted roles second.

Remind yourself that you:

1   Think your own thoughts.

2   Decide your own goals and priorities.

3   Deserve to be treated with respect.

4   Are intelligent, capable and equal to other people.

5   Have a right to react and to express your feelings.

6   Have opinions and values that are as valid as those of other people.

7   Don't need others to make decisions on your behalf. You can say 'yes' or 'no' for yourself.

8   Don't need to make decisions for, or to rescue, other people. They have the right to make their own choices.

9   Will make mistakes – it is a normal part of learning.

10   Will change your mind. Ideas and opinions alter.

11   Can ask if you don't understand something.

12   Have the same right to ask for what you want as other people do.

We are accountable for our own actions and how we respond to other people, but we do not belong to anyone. So we are always free to be ourselves and to look after our personal interests in a fair way. These thoughts will be revisited in actions in Chapter 3.

Why worry?

When preparing to do or say something over which you do not have full control, it is very easy to spend a disproportionate amount of time worrying: over what to say, how to say it, what was said previously, and whether it was right or wrong.

Worrying about *what has passed* will not change what has happened, although focusing on what elements can be improved in future will ensure that things go better next time. Worrying about *what might happen* will not change what is going to happen either, although anticipating problems and difficulties and planning for them will reduce the chance of things going wrong – and your level of worry.

Worrying is generally a waste of energy as it is not constructive or orientated towards problem-solving.

A worry can be turned into something more positive if you focus your concern and turn it into a goal or purpose for action. For example:

The worry: 'I am worried that my son may not settle at his new school, and I am nervous about meeting the teachers and the other parents.'

The solution: 'I will make an effort to get chatting to some of the parents when I drop him off in the mornings.'

The goal: 'I will begin by leaving home early on Monday morning so that I am at the school in good time in order to meet my son's form teacher and familiarize myself with the layout of the school.'

If you are concerned about the consequences should you choose to take action rather than react to a situation, bear in mind that driving the change will increase your confidence levels and your ability to cope with a similar situation in future. Taking action reinforces your ability to deal with situations in a positive way because you become a part of the decision-making process.

Choosing to act

Responding to a situation passively or aggressively implies that you feel powerless to influence the situation. Choosing an assertive response is more involving and shows a willingness and a belief that, if you take action, change can happen on your terms.

In her series, *Confidence Zone*, psychologist Ros Taylor encourages her clients to face their fears by playing the game of 'consequences'. It is a way of looking at the roots and the reality of your concerns and following them through to their ultimate conclusion. If you can look at your greatest fear and think, 'So what? I can handle that!' then your anxiety becomes manageable, or disappears altogether.

If you then look at what would happen if you achieved a *positive* outcome, and follow the same sequence of events, you will be better able to visualize success as a possible outcome as well.

Consequences

Focus on what it is that is undermining your confidence and ask yourself:

'What if the **worst** happened?'

'What would the consequences be?'

_____

'If that happened, then what would be the consequence of that?'

_____

'And the consequence of that happening would be?'

_____

'And the consequence of **that** happening would be?'

_____

'And the next consequence would be?'

_____

And so on and so on, until...

'What would the final outcome be?'

_____

Then ask yourself:

'So what?'

_____

It isn't always necessary to run through the whole sequence. If you can move straight from the 'What if?' to the 'So what?' stage and face the final consequence of your anxiety head-on, it shows that you are able to think positively and take action with sufficient confidence in your ability to handle the outcome.

There is a second stage to the process as well that will reinforce your decision. Once you have got to the root of your concerns, turn it on its head and carry out the same sequence, but this time focus on the consequences of a positive outcome.

Either of these sequences will reinforce your confidence to take action. Doing them both will leave you with very little excuse not to act!

Scenario 1

Fabien wanted to learn to salsa dance, but he was afraid of making a fool of himself.

His negative 'What if?'/'So what?' sequence went like this:
What if I made a fool of myself?
The consequence would be that everyone would laugh at me.
And if everyone laughed at me, I would feel humiliated.
And if I felt humiliated I would never want to see any of those people again.
And if I never saw any of those people again?
So what? I wouldn't mind, as I don't know them anyway.

His positive 'What if?'/'So what?' sequence went like this:
What if I overcame my fear of going to the class?
The consequence would be that I would learn to dance.
And if I learned to dance I would improve my social life.
And if I improved my social life I might find a new girlfriend.
And if I found a new girlfriend...
So what if I feel some fear when I go to class for the first time?!

Having thought the situation through, Fabien realized that his lack of action in taking the first step to 'have a go' was based on a groundless fear that was making him miss out on opportunities that might improve his quality of life.

Scenario 2

Sandra wanted to apply for a promotion in her department at work, but she knew that one of her colleagues was applying too. She believed that he was bound to get the job rather than her, and kept telling herself that there was no point in even going for it.

Her negative 'What if?'/'So what?' sequence went as follows:
What if I applied for the job and didn't get an interview?
I would feel like a failure and everyone would know.
And if everyone knew they would think I was stupid or arrogant to have applied.
And if they thought that about me I would feel even worse.
And if I felt that bad I wouldn't be able to face coming to work.
And if I couldn't face coming to work I would have to look for a new job.
And if I had to look for a new job I might not get an interview.
And if I didn't get an interview I would feel disappointed.
And I would keep trying until I succeeded.
So what? If I am going to feel disappointed about not getting an interview it might as well be for the job I want now.

Her positive 'What if?'/'So what?' sequence went like this:
What if I applied and got the job?
I would be nervous and anxious about my ability to do the job well.

And if I was nervous and anxious I would need to plan and prepare in advance.
And if I needed to plan and prepare, it would be good experience even if I didn't get the job.
So what if I am not successful? I can't stay at this level forever and I can always apply elsewhere.

Having got to the point where she could see that the outcome would be the same whether or not she applied for the role, she could see she had nothing to lose by trying, and might as well be as prepared as possible.

The best weapons to tackle any self-doubt, indecision or concerns about being effective are forward planning, a sense of humour and a sense of perspective. Try on the following thoughts for size:

○ I will plan what I am going to say in advance.
○ Action is better than inaction.
○ I've got nothing to lose by trying, and a lot to lose by not tackling the situation.
○ I will be in the same situation as everyone else.
○ It will be fun/interesting/challenging.
○ It is an opportunity to learn something new.
○ A few moments of embarrassment are better than saying nothing at all.

If the benefits of taking action outweigh the risk of short-term discomfort, then think positive and take action.
However, for some people there is a very fine line between

taking a personal risk and experiencing a feeling of humiliation. If the risks outweigh the personal benefits, don't allow yourself to be coerced by other people into doing something that undermines your sense of self. If it feels right, do it; if it doesn't, don't. It needs to be your decision, and yours alone.

Remember: assertive thinking includes the right to think and say, 'no'.

Where is the evidence?

The brain likes to be proved right. So if you tell yourself that you are good at something then it will look for evidence to support your belief (and vice versa). For example, if you feel that you are a 'hopeless' parent, your thoughts will immediately conjure up instances when your child was upset, rejected your affections, misbehaved, and so on. If, on the other hand, you tell yourself that you are a 'caring and supportive' parent, your brain will be encouraged to think of your child in moments where he or she is happy, smiling, being comforted by, or responsive towards, you. If you are confident in your abilities you will be able to keep both views in perspective and know that effective parenting means a healthy mix of both responses.

However, when confidence or self-esteem is low, negative thoughts and images may quickly crowd out the positive ones. If your negative reactions are deep-rooted, it can be helpful to test the evidence for your beliefs, and to take a reality check to see what is preventing you from moving forwards. The rights and wrongs of a situation are rarely as simple as black and white: shades of grey, differences of opinion, and the benefit of hindsight all play their part.

A reality check will help you to change your perspective on a situation and to look at it from other angles. You may be able to achieve this shift of focus on your own, but it can be invaluable to ask someone you trust to help you to get the 'true' view – especially if you are looking back over time.

Reality check guidelines

1   Where is the evidence?

○ Where is the evidence that supports your current beliefs about yourself or about events that happened in the past?

○ What evidence is there to support the belief that others might be to blame rather than you?

○ Could the reality be the result of a combination of factors? And if so, what are they?

2   Is there an alternative perspective?

○ Who could you ask for an alternative viewpoint?

○ Who would support or challenge your view?

○ Can you trust them to be unbiased?

○ What are their views, and how do they differ from yours?

3   Review the outcomes.

○ What would you do differently next time?

○ What have you learned from the experience?

○ How do you feel, having gone through this process?

4   Plan for action.

○ What do you need to do now to make the situation better?

○ What should you do to ensure it won't happen again?

○ How do you rate your confidence now?

This analysis needn't take a long time. Once you have decided who to ask for a second opinion about the situation, it needn't take more than a focused conversation and a little thinking time to gain some evidence for a different perspective on the situation.

Hugo was bright, charismatic and ambitious, but poor at time management and he tended to put the needs of others ahead of his own. The culture of his department was to stretch people to their limits before bringing in new support staff. Hugo was working long hours and worried about how he would get everything done.

He told himself that he couldn't raise the issue of needing extra staff with his head of department until he had got on top of things. The situation got worse, and the result was that Hugo lost confidence in his ability to deliver work well and on time. Rather than delegate problem projects, he passed on the easy, often high prestige ones. As a result, his section was not only behind, but it became unprofitable too. At the age of 30 his position was made redundant. It was a major blow to his confidence and he was full of regret about not having voiced his needs before the situation reached crisis point.

Five years later, established in another company, the workload was building, and Hugo was getting himself in the same tangle. Although he could see what was happening, he immediately conjured up past demons and told himself he was going to be made redundant. His behaviour began to reinforce his deeply held beliefs, until one day a concerned colleague encouraged him to open up about why he appeared to be self-sabotaging his own success. Hugo explained his fears, and together they discussed the reality of the situation:

1 Where is the evidence?
○ *Hugo drew attention to his inability to get through his workload and to the poor quality of the work he was delivering.*
○ *He pointed to his past redundancy and voiced fears that he saw history repeating itself.*

2 Is there an alternative perspective?
○ *His colleague helped him to see that his work was as good as anyone else's, and that it was his own expectations of failure that were dragging him down.*
○ *He was a valued member of the team and there were others in the team in a worse situation than him.*
○ *The culture of the company was playing its part.*
○ *He pointed out that his former company had had a history of poor financial management. The redundancies were part of a bigger picture. It was the job, not Hugo, that had been made redundant.*

3 Review the outcomes.

○ *Hugo accepted that he had got things out of proportion and he had developed a habit of 'beating himself up' about even the slightest mistake. He was also taking too passive an approach to his current situation.*

○ *He knew the importance of speaking up for himself, and now he needed to put past experience into practice.*

○ *He felt more secure in his role and abilities, but also felt frustrated with himself for not managing matters more effectively.*

4 Plan for action.

○ *He mapped out what he would say to his departmental head, focusing on ways he could contribute more effectively, if he had some practical backup.*

○ *He recognized that his negative thinking needed to be turned around and that he had to put the past behind him, while taking full responsibility for managing his current role and situation.*

○ *He asked his colleague whether he could recommend any tips for managing workload and on speaking to their boss.*

○ *He realized that he felt more confident about himself and his future prospects than he had done for years.*

A progress journal is an ideal place to track your thoughts about this reality check process (see Step 1, p. 51), and it is very useful to write down the results of this exercise. You can't argue with the evidence once it is written down: it is there in black and white for your future reference. Doing this over time will build up an honest picture of how you think and behave in awkward or challenging situations.

It will also help you to be objective about how and when your own thoughts and actions undermine your ability to be assertive.

If you would like to know more about why your thoughts drive your future actions, and the role of your conscious and sub-conscious brain, there are several very interesting books available that will tell you more. One of the leaders in the field of mind and memory is Tony Buzan, whose *Mind Map Book* blazed the trail for many of the inspirational books and techniques that have followed. (See the bibliography for more information.)

Having come to grips with the way you think, the next step is to develop confident ways of expressing yourself. Chapter 3 will begin this process by looking at self-expression and Chapter 4 will follow up by investigating how you communicate with others.

Release your potential – step 2: Think positive

Take responsibility for your thoughts and you will direct your own actions

Our thoughts become our words and our words become our actions, so it is important to think and talk to ourselves in as positive a way as possible. Positive thoughts trigger actions instead of reactions. Once your mind is on track and you have the language to express what you want to say in an assertive fashion, you can't help but communicate more effectively.

Memories are powerful thoughts. A situation or conversation can trigger an unexpected or subconscious memory that results in an instant response – either positive or negative – that may not be relevant to the reality of the present moment.

○ The 'reality check' on p. 71 will help you to determine which of your long-held views of yourself are true and which ones need a change in perspective.

Worrying about the consequences can prevent us from taking the first step towards confident action. Worry is wasted energy, unless it is focused towards preventing or correcting problems.

○ The exercise on p. 66 provides a simple sequence to find out what is at the root of your lack of confidence and help you to take action to become more assertive.

The brain believes what it is told and will seek evidence to back up your thoughts, whether positive or negative. By practising positive thinking techniques you can change your habits from negative to positive and influence your actions too. Part of this process is the need to review past beliefs and to put them in a new and balanced perspective. You are the only person who can take responsibility for your thoughts, your views and your actions.

○ Page 71 describes a four-step exercise for turning false thinking into new and positive action.

③ Express yourself
How to say what you really mean

'Be yourself. Everyone else is already taken.'
OSCAR WILDE

How do you rate your ability to cope with situations confidently? In conversation, do you find it hard to get a word in edgeways, or do you tend to regret having opened your mouth to speak? Do you find yourself thinking of the perfect thing to say after the event? Or do you dominate the conversation and later regret not listening more? Most people find that their confidence in their ability to express themselves ebbs and flows depending on the circumstances, and at vulnerable moments it may feel as if other people have a greater ability to express their opinions than you do.

It is important to have both effective verbal and written skills, because they have a significant impact on your level of success at work and your ability to be yourself. At home and socially, these same communication skills are important for building equal relationships.

If you are thinking confidently then you will know that your views and opinions have value, and that your right to be heard is equal to that of others. Even so, it can be hard to assert yourself without some preparation and practice. Loss of confidence makes us focus inwards, and we become increasingly aware of the physical and nervous sensations inside the body. The more inwardly focused we are, the more isolated and powerless we feel.

This chapter looks at the factors that influence our ability to express ourselves honestly and at the right moment, and offers practical guidance on how to ask questions and say things in ways that ensure you are understood.

Try to recall a moment when you lacked confidence. What were your coping strategies: did you confront the situation or avoid it? What kinds of messages did your senses convey to your brain and how did these transfer to your voice and body language?

Common results include:

○ Anger with yourself for allowing others to get the upper hand.

○ Anger with yourself for getting upset.

○ Increased workload for yourself and raised stress levels.

○ Time and energy wasted thinking and talking about the situation.

○ A blow to self-esteem for not handling the situation effectively.

○ Resentment towards the other person and difficulty in working with or relating to them.

Experiencing these reactions on a regular basis will have a long-term debilitating effect on the body that can impact on your health and well-being. In contrast, being seen to handle a situation well brings personal rewards.

How to grow in confidence

Think about a time when you felt very confident. Again, try to remember what your coping strategies were and how you talked to yourself – especially in moments of acute pressure. How did the messages that you sent to your brain differ from those you sent when you lacked confidence? How could you apply the same tactics to a negative scenario?

Common results include:

○ Pride in your achievements.

○ More efficient working practices and an increase in energy levels.

○ An increase in self-esteem in line with an increase in confidence levels.

○ Positive feelings towards other people.

○ A strong sense of self-belief in your ability to achieve new goals.

Confidence breeds confidence, because with every assertive move you make, the more you will learn to trust and rely on your own knowledge, decision-making and resilience.

Consider the following scenarios

1   You are in a team meeting when one of your colleagues puts forward an idea that you had mentioned to her yesterday. The implication is that it is her idea rather than yours.

2   Your partner belittles you in front of friends by criticizing your method of parking the car. It's not the first time they have done this.

3   Your boss promised you a new job title and a salary increase to go with your increase in responsibilities. She has now been made redundant. Her replacement has a reputation for being fierce and has made it clear that there will be further job cuts.

○ How would you react?
○ When would you respond?
○ What would you say?
○ How would you get the other person to see your point of view?

See the four steps to assertiveness on p. 84 to help you to find the right words to say, at the right time, and with confidence. At times of uncertainty it is possible to be so concerned about how to 'say it right' or 'getting it wrong', that the moment passes and nothing is said at all. Depending on the circumstances, such missed moments can come back to haunt us, and opportunities can pass by, or troubles become more entrenched. If it is hard to act the first time around, it is likely to be harder still the next time – unless you are prepared for action.

Finding the 'right' moment

Although our personality and character remain essentially the same through life, our tastes, opinions and actions will change and evolve, depending on age, influences and experience. 'Stuff happens!' as the phrase goes, and we become adults and continue to grow older; so who we are today will not feel the same as who we were yesterday – and it will change again in the future. That's why waiting until 'the moment is right' to speak up (for something you believe in, to voice an opinion, or to break difficult news) is usually a mistake. The moment may *never* be right; you have to *create* your own 'right moment' and manage the discussion in a positive way.

It can be especially difficult to act assertively and clearly if you are conscious of the knock-on effect of your actions on someone else – your child, for example.

Jenny had lived in the UK – away from her family in Hong Kong – since she was a teenager at boarding school. All of the family were high achievers, and there was every expectation that Jenny would perform well at school – which she did. High grades allowed her a choice of universities. Jenny wanted to become a teacher, but her parents disapproved of this idea and encouraged her instead to study commerce and economics. Jenny knew that they had her best interests at heart and so complied with their wishes. Their strong hope was that she would return to Hong Kong to build her career.

While at university in Scotland, Jenny learned to make her own choices and to try new experiences. Her normally passive approach changed and she became more outgoing; she felt comfortable with her new persona and happy with her life. She also met the man who would become her husband. He was a teacher, and he re-awoke her own desire to be a primary school teacher. Never a rebellious child, and aware of the high hopes her parents had for her, she lacked the confidence to tell them about her relationship, her boyfriend's profession, and the fact that she wanted to change her course. The dread of her family's disapproval and her personal guilt at 'letting them down' began to eat into her new-found confidence. She kept waiting for the right moment to break her news, but while she did so she became so depressed by her inability to express her needs that her grades slumped and her tutors began to question whether she would graduate. Jenny was at crisis point: in danger of having to return to her parents' home with no qualifications, losing her relationship and, as she saw it, having no future. She no longer knew who she was and had retreated into passive 'escape' behaviour.

Fortunately her boyfriend was sensitive to her situation and he helped her to face her fears, analyze the situation from both sides and plan what she was going to say before she picked up the phone to speak to her parents. In this way she was able to create an appropriate 'moment', as well as seize the initiative, presenting her situation in a positive way that did not disregard their feelings.

The outcome was not plain sailing, and the discussions were not without their distressing moments, but her parents came to respect her decision and supported her choices. She gained a 2.1 in her degree in Economics, and stayed on a further year to earn top accolades as a trainee teacher as well.

Many of our choices and actions in life will affect other people and we should remain aware of, and take responsibility for, that. However, importantly, the results of our choices will also impact on us: they will influence how we think, how we feel about ourselves and, ultimately, what drives us into action to achieve our goals or to change approach in the future.

Four steps to assertiveness

Stress symptoms related to lack of assertiveness can take over at inappropriate moments. Some people become obviously nervous – others become loud or defensive, over-flamboyant or unfocused. A sense of not being heard can be disguised by behaviour such as shouting, sulking or inner withdrawal from the situation. The good news is that many of these responses can be 'unlearned' and turned into positive communication techniques.

There are four elements to communicating assertively:

1   Understanding the other person's point of view.

2   Expressing your own feelings or thoughts about the situation.

3   Proposing solutions or stating what you would like to happen.

4   Asking for opinions or feedback.

No matter how emotional you are feeling, try to stay calm and follow each of these steps by using a neutral but emphatic voice and open body language. (More about this in Chapter 5.)

Understanding the other person's point of view

First, you will need to show the person (or people) that you are speaking to that you understand, or have taken into account, their views.

Sentences might start with:

'I realize that...'

'I understand that...'

'I can see that...'

This approach will help to get the other person onside; they will not need to adopt a defensive stance because you have already shown them that you are listening. If your voice is calm, then they will tend to be calm in response. If your body language is neither defensive nor aggressive, they will probably mirror your approach.

Expressing your own feelings or thoughts about the situation

The next step is to explain how you are feeling about their viewpoint. Remember – you have a right to disagree or to see things differently to others. It is possible to respect another person's right to an opinion without either agreeing with or alienating them.

Sentences that show how you feel might start with:

'I feel that...'

'I think that...'

In this way you are taking responsibility for feeling the way you do and you are conveying very clearly where you stand. You are asking the person you are speaking to to listen to you with the same courtesy and consideration that you have shown them.

Proposing solutions or stating what you would like to happen

The third step is to build on their understanding of your feelings and point of view by suggesting a proposal, an action or a solution:

> *'I want...'*
> *'I'd like...'*
> *'How about...?'*

The advantage of this approach is its clarity. You are not asking anyone to guess or intuit what you want; there is no opportunity for misunderstanding and disagreement later; you are stating clearly and calmly what your preferences are.

Asking for opinions or feedback

But, of course, communication is a two-way process and assertive conversations need to respect the needs of everyone involved. So the fourth step is to ask for a response:

> *'What do you think?'*

This approach does not automatically mean that you will get the response you wanted, or hoped for; but it does mean that there is a calm and fair environment in which to have a conversation or a reasoned discussion.

Finding your voice

Once you have taken time to consider and understand the underlying reasons for your anxiety about your communication skills (see Chapter 1), and have built the habit of positive thinking and positive speech into your daily life (see Chapter 2), you will be ready to find your true voice.

We often make the mistaken assumption that other people are motivated by the same things as we are, and we take actions and make decisions based on presumptions about what other people want – only to discover that we have got it wrong. This is most likely to happen at home, when parents make decisions for their children or partners make decisions for each other. However, it can happen at work as well – especially if the image we portray to others contradicts our true persona and ambitions.

It is wise never to make decisions that affect other people without first asking them for their opinion and establishing what they want. Hearing afterwards that you got it wrong, when your action was taken with the best of intentions, can be uncomfortable and awkward for all parties. Likewise, the only person who knows what is right for you, is you.

For those of you who are soft-spoken, too shy to be heard, or uncomfortable at the sound of your voice, the following exercise is designed to break down your natural levels of reserve and to find the 'inner you' – who is just dying to shout out!

The 'over the top' exercise

Ideally you should film yourself working through this exercise on a video camera or similar, so that you can watch your body language afterwards. Choose two other people to do this exercise with you, so that you have one person working with you and at least one other to judge the event and act as the audience. It doesn't matter who they are, how old they are and whether you know them or not!

You are all going to speak for one minute on a topic of choice:

❍ The topic should be foolish: toothbrushes, runner beans, paper clips, house bricks. This is so that there can be no misconception that the content is in any way important.

❍ All participants must speak at the same time.

❍ The winner is the one that outpaces and outperforms the other by grabbing the attention of the audience.

❍ A vote can be taken to judge the winner.

A no-pressure, fun situation like this encourages people to push themselves beyond their usual boundaries, to feel less inhibited about shouting and speaking up (because they are not being judged), and as a result their true character will show through.

If a video has been used, review performance to see how body language and voice projection contribute to the 'winning' performance.

Most people find that, having released their 'voice' in public, and seeing how emphatic they come across on screen, there is no longer as much need to hide behind a more introspective persona to make yourself heard.

(*Confidence Zone*, p. 34.)

The art of asking questions

Confidence and assertiveness skills are essential if you are to feel comfortable socially. Developing the skill of being able to talk to people you have never previously met, in a way that encourages *them* to talk, is crucial to building new friendships, as well as to creating and maintaining business contacts.

Generally speaking, we choose to do business with people that we like, and we like people who are easy to talk to. So it makes sense to learn how to make the most of conversation, so that you can really connect with people. It's not just what we say and how we say it that are important, it also matters which questions we choose to ask. Questions can be conversation openers or conversation stoppers; they can make people feel interrogated or appreciated; they are a tool that can be used to draw people out, find out specific details, or end a conversation.

In broad terms there are three styles of questions:

○ *Closed questions* prompt short, factual answers that provide facts, but do not broaden understanding or invite conversation. They can also be used to end a conversation or close a deal.

○ *Open questions* signal that the questioner is interested in what you have to say. They begin with words such as which, where and who. The person answering is being given *carte blanche* to say or give away as much or as little as they choose. These questions are used to open up a conversation and to learn more about the person and what motivates them.

○ *Probing questions* are used by the questioner to take the person deeper and more specifically into their subject. They are used to verify the generalizations made in an open answer, and designed to draw out someone who has withdrawn into closed replies.

Types of questions

Closed	Open	Probing
Are?	What?	How?
Do?	Which?	In what way?
Have?	Where?	Tell me more...
	Who?	Describe in more detail...
	Why?	For what reasons?

If you are already comfortable talking to people you don't know, then you probably use these different styles in daily conversation quite naturally. Anyone who is less at ease would find it valuable to practise and listen for them in order to get a sense of how conversation ebbs and flows. It can be very useful on occasion to be in conscious control of the way that a conversation develops, especially in business. If you are involved in sales, a stylized conversation might go like this:

How can I help you?
(Probing: 'Is the person interested in what I'm selling?')
What are you looking for?
(Open: 'What does this person really want? What are their buying triggers?')
Would you want to buy today?
(Closed: 'How serious a purchaser are they?')

A softer, social example is as follows:
Where did you go on holiday?
(Open: could give a one-word or half-hour answer.)
What are the sports facilities like there?
(Probing: inviting further detail.)
Would you want to go back again in future?
(Closed: a 'yes' or 'no' reply likely.)

Partially preparing the kinds of things you might say before going somewhere you may find daunting – such as to a dinner party, an office lunch or important client meeting – can make all the difference between feeling relaxed during the event or worrying about what you're going to say the whole time.

Of course, conversations are about content too, so be prepared to ask people some general questions. If you're at a business meeting, these can be kept general – in terms of professional background, the state of the market, or how new projects that the company is involved in might be going.

There are fewer boundaries for social conversation.

Everyone has a family; most have hobbies; everyone was born somewhere or lived somewhere – so you will have some common ground to talk about. When in doubt, ask questions and listen. It is a cliché, but true, that with an attentive audience most people are happy to talk about themselves!

Be aware of how you use your body language. It can either draw people towards you or push them away. (See Chapter 5 for more details.)

By mastering the art of asking questions you will develop your own conversational style.

Your right to say 'no'

There is another important aspect to finding your own voice: knowing when to say 'no'. Boundaries are important; in life and in relationships. If you find it hard to say 'no' to people, or to disagree with them in a calm manner, you need to check your thinking (see Chapter 2) and remind yourself of your rights as an individual (see p. 63).

Remember that:

❍ You have the right to say 'no'.

❍ Your opinions are as valid as anyone else's.

❍ You have the right to be listened to.

❍ You have the right to criticize in a constructive manner if someone has not behaved as or delivered what was promised.

❍ You have the right to be spoken to with respect.

If you find that you say 'yes' to other people's requests

more often than you say 'no', and that you are usually the person who agrees to help others out of habit, these guidelines may be more of a challenge to adapt to.

If you're keeping a progress journal, use it to anticipate and become aware of the areas where you are particularly vulnerable. Who do you find it hard to say 'no' to? Could you speak to them at a time when they are not approaching you for assistance to tell them that you find it hard to say 'no', and to give them dates or times when it would be more convenient to help out? Or, alternatively, practise explaining that, although you've been happy to help up until now, it will no longer be possible to offer that support. Most people will respect an honest explanation. Remember to focus on the task or the favour, and not the person, in order to avoid making the recipient feel that they are being criticized.

How to say 'no'

Here are some top tips for saying the 'no' word the confident way:

❍ Ask for more information before committing yourself to something you're unsure about.

❍ Say, 'I am unsure and need time to think. I will come back to you.' (But make sure you do!)

❍ Practise saying 'no' in a simple and unembellished way.

❍ Don't apologize for saying 'no'.

❍ Do feel you can walk away after saying 'no'.

❍ Do feel able to explain your feelings about saying 'no'.

For example: 'I feel awkward saying 'no', but it just isn't

convenient'; 'I feel annoyed at having to say 'no' again';
'I thought I had explained my reasons clearly last time we
spoke'.

○ Be honest with yourself. Say 'no' upfront, rather than
saying 'yes' and then changing your mind at the last
minute.

○ Make sure your body language is echoing your message:
for example, arms crossed, frowning, shaking head
(rather than smiling or nodding and giving contradictory
messages).

○ If you want to end a conversation, stand up. It is a signal
that the discussion is over.

Developing the ability to express your opinions honestly,
without fearing what other people might say or think, is a
crucial part of acting confidently. If you are true to yourself
habitually you will learn to become comfortable being
yourself, whatever the situation. It also makes life easier for
other people, who can be confident that they understand
your position. Deciding what you want to say will come far
more easily with practice and will have a positive impact
on yourself as well as on those around you.

Handling criticism and compliments

Few people find it easy to take criticism lightly, but those
who have a strong sense of self will find it easier to see the
value in having constructive feedback.

Criticism comes in many forms. At its best it is
constructive, objective, and designed to help improve

performance or behaviour. In contrast, critical words spoken in the heat of the moment or expressed with mixed motives can be undermining, vicious and counter-productive. We will all experience criticism during our lives and know that in a negative context it triggers feelings of:

○ being unloved
○ disapproval
○ punishment
○ hurt
○ fear of rejection.

Our responses to coming under attack are usually inwardly or outwardly defensive. Our language, expressions and body language will say:

Outwardly	**Inwardly**
I don't care.	It's not my fault.
It's not fair.	You never see the good things.
I can't help it.	Poor me.

The baseline rule for passing criticism or giving feedback is to comment on the behaviour, not the person. Unfortunately, many people tend to forget this – especially during personal arguments at home and in relationships. As soon as someone is put under attack, they will go on the defensive. Their reactions may be immediate or slow-burning, aggressive or passive. An aggressive response may exacerbate the situation, but at least feelings are out in the open and dealt with. The passive response may be ultimately more damaging.

If you have a tendency to blame yourself, or to believe any criticism that is thrown at you, the key rule is: avoid the temptation to accept every comment without question.

For example: your partner throws the comment at you that, 'Things always have to be done on your terms.' An apology is inappropriate at this point and won't get to the bottom of the issue if the criticism is unfounded. Instead, acknowledge that he or she is upset and ask for clarification.

An assertive response will acknowledge the problem, allow you to accept blame if necessary and let you explain how you feel about the criticism. Suggest a solution; ask for feedback; and focus first on the other person rather than you:

'I've obviously upset you [Acknowledgement] and that makes me feel terrible [Feelings]. Can we talk about it so that we can avoid a repeat situation [Solution]? What do you say [Feedback]?'

Ask yourself whether the statement is a valid criticism or whether the comment is disguising a deeper and different issue.

If the criticism is valid, the assertive and fair response would be to acknowledge your mistake:

'I can see why you feel that way. It's the second time in a fortnight that I have had to reschedule dinner, and that is hurtful. Could we make a firm arrangement for two weeks' time? My work commitments will have eased off by then.'

By taking responsibility for your own mistakes or actions, you act assertively. It allows everyone involved to choose to put the event behind them and move on. If you are being falsely accused, resist the impulse to take the comment on board, to apologize in order to gain a quiet life, or to lose your temper. Practise refuting such comments calmly but firmly:

'That is an unfair comment. I do not expect things to be always on my terms. You know that the emergency at the office meant I had to make work my priority during the last two weeks. Is there something else that is troubling you?'

If you are receiving comments that contain hidden or implied criticism, don't be afraid to tackle the situation head-on, using a non-aggressive and balanced, assertive approach. Ask outright what the problem is and be specific in your questioning:

'Have I...?'
'Are you...?'
'Do you feel...?'

None of us is faultless, and criticism is a useful way to get direct feedback that we can learn from constructively for the future. After all, the only way we can ascertain how to do things better and more effectively is by making mistakes, and by learning from them.

Desensitization

Each of us has weak spots that can act as quick-fire touchpapers in moments of vulnerability. Personal comments about an aspect of our looks, background, origins, religion, professional competence, loved ones, or character can trigger deeply held hurts and irrational responses. Being aware of these weak spots in our make-up can help us to learn to deal with them before they catch us out.

Desensitization works by exposing ourselves to the cause of our anxiety more and more frequently, so that it gradually diminishes in importance until it becomes of little or no threat at all. Some people find visualization techniques are helpful in achieving this. Start by imagining that you are being constantly exposed to an awkward or painful scenario, and then imagine yourself dealing with it in a constructive and positive way. This may feel uncomfortable to begin with, but repeat the exercise and its outcome at least 20 to 30 times, until you feel in control of the situation and no longer defensive.

Desensitization can also be practised with a friend or family member who understands what you want to achieve and whom you can trust to have your best interests at heart.

In general:

○ Avoid being over-apologetic.

○ Use your tone of voice to convey personal conviction.

○ Don't allow your feelings to build up. It will be harder to keep your emotions in check if you do.

Fear of 'losing it', in tears or temper, holds many people back from walking through their manager's door, or phoning a friend, to have a frank conversation about an issue that has triggered the negative response.

Accepting compliments

People who lack assertiveness skills in other areas are often surprisingly firm when batting back compliments, declaring that they are not worthy of them.

A compliment about work may be met with 'Did you notice my mistake?' or, 'It could have been so much better' or, 'I doubt anyone else will think so'.

A compliment about looking great with a new haircut, dress or suit, could be met with 'You're joking, I feel an absolute wreck' or, 'I really must go on a diet. Look how tight it is' or, 'It's only a cheap bargain that I got in the sales'.

Elise never felt particularly good about her looks and had perfected her habit of rejecting compliments, until one day a friend challenged her response with: 'For once, why can't you just say "Thank you"? You don't have to agree with me, and I don't need a lecture. I am offering you a compliment; I am sharing my opinion and I would like you to respect it.'

Elise realized in that moment that rejecting compliments or batting them back to the giver is an inadvertent putdown for the other person. A compliment with no alternative motive is a real gift and a practical endorsement of something you have done well – if you choose to look at it that way.

Putting it all together

You can't expect to change your behaviour overnight, but with practice, determination and the willingness to accept feedback from others, it is possible to get to a position where you are far more comfortable about making the first move to speak to someone new, to lead conversations and to believe that you can make a difference by speaking up.

The following chapter looks at putting together making an impact: how you think and how you speak, as well as working with other people.

Release your potential – step 3: Talk positive

Say what you mean, mean what you say and choose to say it

Being yourself in all situations is the key to 'saying it right' and saying it with confidence. If you are not naturally confident speaking to other people, either one-to-one or in a group, you will need to practise your skills until the techniques become second nature. Know yourself, and plan what you're going to say. Don't *wait* for the 'right' moment; *create* the 'right' moment.

Use the four steps to assertive behaviour:

❍ Understand the other person
❍ Express your feelings
❍ Propose solutions
❍ Seek feedback

If you're not being heard there may be a reason! Push yourself to find your voice.

❍ The exercise on p. 88 is a fun but powerful way to see yourself in action.

The art of asking questions is at the heart of speaking with confidence: to listen and also to be heard are the keys to assertive communication.

The section starting on p. 89 will help you to practise open, probing and closed questions so that you are in a position to drive, rather than react to, conversations and new meetings.

How to take action

Bringing about lasting change in your communication habits is about more than reading the theory; it needs full-scale commitment to practise communication techniques. Reading over Steps 1, 2, and 3 of the book so far, revisit what you would like to achieve and what you would like to be different about your personal style.

Using your communication journal – if you are keeping one – or by simply getting it down on paper, write down the following points for action:

❍ What I'm going to start doing, and by when.

❍ What I'm going to stop doing, and when.

❍ When I am going to review my progress (list date and times).

❍ I will know that I have succeeded when (state goal).

Commit to starting this action plan now, and decide when you are going to revisit it for a reality check. Once you are more comfortable with being yourself, and guiding yourself, you will be more comfortable learning to apply those skills to influencing other people.

4 Speaking up

How to communicate with others

'If I am to speak ten minutes, I need a week for preparation; if fifteen minutes, three days; if half an hour, two days; if an hour, I am ready now.'

WOODROW WILSON

Communicating with just one person differs from talking with a group of people, or from presenting information in a more formal situation, because when talking one-to-one, especially to someone you know well, it is possible to judge mood, read body language and assess the other person's reactions to your words, face to face. You can adjust your tone, style or what you are saying as necessary, and quickly, depending on their responses. It doesn't necessarily mean the conversation is easy, but it does mean you can be confident that your reading of the situation is fairly accurate.

Talking to groups or a senior colleague, chairing meetings, managing teams, making presentations and other scenarios where you need to be influential, is often challenging for other reasons:

○ It is impossible to maintain eye contact with everyone in the room.

○ You need to hold everyone's attention.

○ You are expected (in whatever detail) to know what you are talking about.

○ You cannot tell what people are thinking.

○ You are 'on show' with nowhere to hide.

○ You are vulnerable to criticism.

○ You can't please all of the people all of the time.

○ You feel you are being judged.

○ The 'group' may appear as a formidable whole, instead of as a collection of individuals in your mind.

○ You may feel out of control.

○ You may fear making a fool of yourself.

○ Assessing and changing the mood of a group, in particular, is a more challenging process.

Feeling anxious in such a situation is natural. A person who is otherwise rational, articulate and confident can be reduced to nervous inaction at the prospect of making a difficult phone call, voicing criticism, or talking to a group of people – whether known or unknown.

The keys to overcoming this apprehension are:

○ *Self-awareness* – Be aware of how you feel about what you are going to say. How do you want to come across to your audience?

○ *Positive thinking* – Check your thinking is supporting, not undermining, you.

○ *Preparation* – The better prepared you are, the more self-confident you will feel.

○ *Listening* – Being attentive to comments and feedback

will involve others while also taking the pressure off you to perform.

○ *Focus* – Concentrate on what you are saying and how people respond to you.

○ *Clarity* – Be clear about what you are trying to achieve and state things unambiguously.

○ *Honesty* – Don't try to dress up your feelings. State things as they are. It's possible to be honest without being rude or over-emotional – and it enables people to know exactly where they stand.

Self-awareness is your starting point. How do you feel about the situation, and why? What do you want to say? How do you want to come across? (See Chapter 1.)

Check your thinking. If your thoughts are supporting your goals in a positive way, then you will stand a better chance of making things happen confidently – and to handle a situation well if something goes wrong.

The better prepared you are, the more in control you will feel and the more assured you will sound when you state your opinions and choices. Preparation means anticipating what others are going to say and feeling 'one step ahead of the game'. Plan ahead so that you know exactly what you are trying to say. If it is an important or sensitive conversation, think through in advance the various directions in which the discussion might go, and be ready to answer awkward questions or have an opinion in relation to core issues.

When preparing yourself to speak, consider also

what your personal boundaries might be. If you are going for an interview, do you hold any views that might be in conflict with the company's ethos? If you are applying for a promotion, are you *au fait* with the department's strategic plans for development? Perhaps a business event includes having dinner with a business colleague you happen to find difficult. Do you need to decide in advance how you will respond if the conversation becomes uncomfortable or challenging?

As the saying goes: you have two ears and one mouth, so use them accordingly. The more you can hone your listening skills, the better people will respond to you and the more appropriate your responses will be. Encourage people to speak and to contribute by asking open questions (see p. 89) and by making clear your own interest or objective too. Be aware if someone is avoiding giving you a clear answer. Effective listening means being discerning too.

If you are focused and clear in expressing your feelings, it will be easier for others to understand what it is that you want. State calmly what you would prefer to happen and what you require to make that happen. If two people hold differing views, you may need to be a mediator, without alienating either one of them.

Be honest about your own needs and resist the temptation to try to please or protect others from the reality of the situation. The following scenario shows how this might happen:

Clive: 'I haven't been able to complete the report for this morning's meeting because there was a power cut last night.' (Bluffer's excuse)

Tony: 'But you knew that we needed the material this morning (alerting to his responsibility). *Why didn't you plan to finish it two days ago?*' (Alerting to the need to set goals)

Clive: 'I did, but my girlfriend's in hospital and I've been so worried...' (Serious excuse)

Tony: (Cutting through the excuses.) '*I totally understand. It's been a difficult week for you.* (Empathy) *If you'd like to take a few days off to be with her, please let me know.*' (Solution)

'*The lack of a report does leave me with an immediate problem though.* (Alerting to own problem) *If I can move the meeting to this afternoon* (Solution) *could you use the next two hours to finish it?* (Time-bound direction) *I'd value your knowledge and would rather not delegate it to anyone else at this stage.*' (Positive feedback)

Clive: 'Yes, I can do that – and I would like to take the rest of the week off.'

Tony: 'That's great – and yes, of course. But if there is anything else on your desk that is outstanding, please come and discuss it before you go.' (No more excuses)

Tony has listened to Clive and shown him that he understands his situation – but that he needs to manage his work priorities because his behaviour is having a negative effect on others. Importantly, he criticized the behaviour, not the person. The use of positive feedback has the benefit of keeping Clive motivated and preventing the reprimand from undermining his personal confidence.

Exactly the same process and considerations should be applied to relationships at home.

The value of praise

People will always respond more positively to praise than to criticism; it is the key to nurturing self-confidence in others and is a cornerstone of positive personal development. Just as talking positively to yourself will encourage positive performance, so too speaking positively to others feeds their inner voice and ensures that they will also raise their game.

How to give praise

○ Give praise as soon as it's due – it has more power in the moment of success. Don't save it up for a rainy day.
○ Be specific rather than general. Say, 'I think your painting is vibrant and colourful' rather than, 'That's good'.
○ If there are likely to be positive consequences if they continue a certain behaviour, then let them know and encourage them to keep doing it: 'I think you would have a chance of winning the regional art competition with painting of that calibre.' It should also inspire the setting of future goals.
○ Avoid gushing or exaggeration as it will only undermine your words. Keep your praise honest, sincere and to the point.

Seek to give praise as often, or more often, than you criticize – even if there is room for improvement. Encouragement breeds confidence and better performance.

Dealing with difficult people

Unfortunately, praise is not the only style of feedback we need to present with confidence. From time to time a difficult situation rears its head that demands constructive criticism and a firm approach.

Never ignore a people-problem. It won't go away – instead it will just get worse.

We all come up against people who we find difficult to cope with. Why one person is a challenge when another isn't is not always immediately clear. (See p. 84 for points to consider if you feel your response is more instinctive than rational and you need to find a more balanced approach.) It's important to remember that you have an equal right to speak up and make your views known (see p. 63). You also need to resist allowing anyone to have greater influence over you than you have over yourself. A person whose behaviour is difficult can assume great importance in your mind and both the problem and the person can become larger than they really are. In order to talk to him or her assertively, it's important to put yourself on an equal footing.

In a work situation 'difficult' people tend to be those who prevent us in some way from getting the job done.

They might be people who block progress, procrastinate, moan, are aggressive, worry too much, or just don't deliver what they've promised. At home and socially, the influence of a 'difficult person' may be more subtle and harder to acknowledge. Labelling one of your nearest and dearest as 'difficult' is not a constructive thing to do, but nevertheless a person close to you may be having a negative impact on you and your life. Whereas at work it may be possible to work around or avoid confronting someone you find awkward, at home it is vital to approach the situation head-on, and to have a frank conversation about how their unwelcome behaviour is affecting you. If you ignore it there is a danger that the pattern will continue and the impact will be worse further down the line.

The following steps are very useful in preparing yourself to speak up and regain confidence – and initiative.

○ Review the assertiveness guidelines on p. 84 and plan what you are going to say.

○ Before speaking to the difficult person in question, whether by phone or face to face, take several deep breaths and make sure that you are feeling calm and well-prepared to manage the situation.

○ Make a list of key points for discussion. In that way if anyone attempts to take you off on a less important tangent, you can state 'I have something else I would like to ask you first' and bring them back to where you want to be.

○ Don't allow the conversation to become free-form and a launchpad for minor grievances.

○ If the conversation gets too heated, gain space by suggesting that you reconvene or call back.

Kate has run her own business successfully for more than ten years. She talks about the aspect she finds the hardest to manage:

'I find it a challenge to deal with difficult people. By difficult I mean those whose behaviour ranges from aggressive to evasive. I can hold strong opinions myself, and I know it can be hard for others to get a word in edgeways when I'm in mid-flow. Seeing how people deal with me has helped me cope with others.

If someone is 'het up' or passionate about something I just let them speak (if time allows). I've discovered that the best thing to do is let them roll until they have run out of steam. There's no point in trying to interrupt, because they will be so intent on expressing their own opinions that they won't be focused on what I have to say anyway.

I also find that actively listening while the person has their say puts you in a stronger position, because you're being given so much information: a response to your issues; a picture of their issues; and everything else in between. Once they have finished speaking they are more ready to listen, because you've given them time and space to speak, and you can then rightly claim the floor.

I then try to focus discussion on just the core issues – and not get distracted by the rest. If the person I am speaking to has other issues to talk about, I arrange a time for discussion on another occasion. If they have a preferred solution then I ask them for that too – and ask them to give me time to think.'

There is a natural tendency in most people to avoid, evade or ignore difficult people and situations; but there is really only one law of success in a tricky situation, and that is to take a deep breath, take your courage in both your hands and to look the situation in the face. Plan for it, stand up to it – but don't run away from it. If you take the initiative you will increase your ability to manage people as well as your levels of confidence.

The same approach is true if *you* are the one who is being difficult. If you're conscious of having let someone down, or know that something that you have done has gone wrong, you may feel nervous that you will be subjected to someone's anger.

A useful way to deal with this effectively is to face up to your personal responsibility for what has gone wrong, and to phone or face the person with the problem. Nine times out of ten an honest apology that acknowledges blame (especially if it is accompanied by a satisfactory solution) will be accepted graciously. By taking control of the situation and facing up to your own errors, you will automatically increase your confidence in your ability to handle such situations – and hopefully reduce the chance of a repeat event. (However, constant apologies and a repeating pattern of unsatisfactory behaviour will have an opposite and negative effect, of course.)

Losing emotional control

There are times in all our lives when we feel tired, emotional, low and unable to cope; at other times the emotion may be anger, irritation or disappointment. Whatever the scenario, if you find yourself getting emotional and know that your confidence is fading, try not to give in to your feelings there and then.

If you are with other people, take the initiative and explain that you need to take a short break. The pause will help you to regain self-control before returning to talk further in a more confident manner.

If, on the other hand, it is clear that the discussion is going nowhere, suggest that you *both* (or all) take 'time out' and reconvene to discuss the core issues at a newly allocated time. Suggest that you exchange information about the points of concern before you meet – to give both sides a chance to prepare. Emphasize that the aim will be to review the situation from both (or all) points of view.

Richard runs a small team and is actively involved in various committees in his local area. He has another point to make:

'Empathy is important,' he says. 'It is easy to become so entrenched in your own point of view that you dismiss another's standpoint. I have been guilty of discounting what people are saying if it doesn't match my point of view; but you have to take the opinions of others on board. My advice would be, as far as possible, to begin a conversation with a positive

view of what the other person is saying. Flexibility and understanding in a discussion situation are important, even when you're under pressure.'

Being flexible is not the same as being compliant, however. If you feel you are being bamboozled by someone who is not as keen to achieve a 'win-win' situation as you are, hold firm. Feel confident that you can continue to repeat and rephrase your view calmly for as long as it takes for the other person to start to listen.

How to brainstorm ideas

Brainstorming is a wonderful way to find out what people are really thinking and to stretch accepted boundaries. Although used mainly as a group communication tool in a work situation, brainstorming can be used at home as well – it's a great way to find out what your kids or partner really feel about going on holiday, your decorating plans, your family's future, and so on.

The key to effective brainstorming in a group is to keep the tone light and to ensure that everyone feels able to contribute without worrying that they may make a mistake. Explain the aims of the brainstorming session in advance, and describe clearly and succinctly what you want people to do. The group will then take on its own momentum.

○ Go for quantity of ideas, not quality.
○ Don't judge contributions – there are no right or wrong answers.

- Keep the momentum going at a steady pace.
- Make connections between ideas.
- Keep everyone involved.

There can be a tendency for some people to dominate or to make louder contributions to a discussion than others. If this starts to happen, work around the group and encourage everyone to have their say.

Once the brainstorming session is completed, ask each person (or group) to select their best idea. Create a separate list of 'best' ideas and give each person two ticks that they can allocate to either one or to two choices. The idea with the greatest number of ticks is the group's preferred favourite.

In this way, each person is given an equal say and can speak out confidently to voice their ideas with no fear of criticism. The added benefit is that everyone in the group is bound to buy in to the ideas because they created them; they weren't thrust upon them.

Managing meetings

In a similar way to a brainstorming session, a meeting should pool together everyone's ideas and generate feedback. The difference in a meeting situation is that the shape and pace of the discussion is driven by an agenda. A confident chair should manage the boundaries of the meeting while making sure that all the relevant parties have their say.

A meeting will be easier to manage and more

successful in its outcome if you speak to each person one-to-one before the meeting starts. This allows you to find out what people's opinions are, to offer your own point of view, and to be better prepared to manage any situations that arise face to face.

Points of view should be debated and encouraged, but if confrontations occur that are unconstructive, state clearly that the difference of opinion will need to be resolved outside the meeting in order not to hold up progress. Use the group to help you if necessary – if an individual is being awkward, the others will want the awkwardness to stop as much as you.

Giving presentations

For many people, the prospect of giving a presentation, making a speech, or simply standing in front of a group of people to say thank you, will mean sleepless nights, pre-performance nerves and other symptoms of anxiety.

Feeling nervous is normal, and is the body's way of increasing adrenaline levels prior to performance in order to help you decide whether to face or flee the situation. The keys to confident behaviour are preparation, rehearsal and self-belief.

The following comments are typical of the feelings of many people who suffer nerves when making presentations:

Jane: 'The thing I hate is the utter silence – and then the solitary sound of my own voice. My brain goes numb and I feel completely detached from what I am saying or how I'm saying it. All I can hear is my quiet, monotone voice – and I become certain that everyone is bored to death!'

Paul: 'I'm not very good at thinking on my feet, so I write everything down and then either lose my way, or I become so glued to my notes that there is no spontaneity. I would love to be one of those people who can just stand up and speak.'

Eric: 'I try to keep my notes to a minimum to encourage myself just to talk. But my mind just goes blank. It's as if I have never had an idea in my head – and then I panic. I am totally incapable of improvisation!'

To help you to prime yourself ahead of the event:

❍ Preparation is everything and counts for at least 80 per cent of your overall success. Knowing that you are prepared will help to improve your levels of confidence and self-assurance too.

❍ Anticipate awkward questions, and practise your answers in advance.

❍ Take a few minutes to breathe and relax before you begin to speak.

❍ Avoid the temptation to drink alcohol before the event.

❍ Dress appropriately (and comfortably).

❍ If possible, meet with your audience informally in advance. This will help you to build a connection and to break the group down into individuals in your mind.

❍ Always assume that the audience wants to listen to what you have to say.

❍ Introduce yourself, and the topic.

Speaking up

❍ Know your audience and adjust your words and tone accordingly.

❍ Involve people from the audience – either directly or by referring to them and inviting their contribution.

❍ Use eye contact.

❍ Be yourself – and use your own style.

If the sound of silence fills you with panic, or you don't like the sound of your own voice, practise in your own home or at the office until you are more used to hearing it. You don't hear your voice as others hear it, so it sounds unfamiliar and different from the sound of the voice inside your head. Recording yourself and listening to your delivery will help you to improve your style. Avoid being over-critical. If you find yourself using words like 'terrible', 'awful', and so on, to describe your voice, apply the reality check technique outlined on p. 71 and ask someone else for their point of view.

Meg runs a department within a multinational firm. She often has to make presentations, which still fill her with anxiety. Her greatest fear is drying up halfway through and forgetting what she wants to say.

'I used to be so anxious about presentations that it became a self-fulfilling prophecy,' she says. 'Then a friend told me that his way of handling such moments is to pause, make eye contact with others in the room, and to ask questions. It may feel a nerve-wracking thing to do – especially if your brain has seized up at an awkward moment – but no one will remember in retrospect

exactly when or why you paused. They will, however, recall having the opportunity to voice an opinion. Asking questions engages people at a much deeper level and ensures they are listening to what you have to say. It also allows you to unfreeze your mind and to get back on track in a more appropriate way.'

The assertive parent

All the techniques recommended in this book can be applied as easily at home as in an office situation, and those who may benefit more than most are parents and their children.

Children and teenagers need space to establish their personal identities, and will often push the boundaries of behaviour to test your limits as well as their own. Finding ways to communicate positively with your kids is crucial, even when they are straining your patience.

Similar rules to those described above for a business presentation apply to a family situation. Treat your children, and their views, with respect. They are learning about the world and they need to be allowed to make mistakes in order to learn from them and to develop their own confident behaviour. That's not to say that a free-for-all is the wise way forward, though – and there times when some assertive talking is needed to re-establish boundaries and mutual respect.

Lisa and Tom were having great difficulty communicating with their 15-year-old son Jake. Jake was using the house more like a hostel than a home and had turned challenging their authority into an art form. He practised playing his electric guitar loudly, brought friends home at all hours, raided the fridge of anything and everything, and his room was becoming impassable as it was such a smelly and untidy tip. Communication had broken down on all sides; moody silences, door slamming and shouting had become the norm. Tom was particularly concerned about the aggressive way in which Jake spoke to Lisa, who was outwardly passive but inwardly highly distressed by her son's disregard. She often became tearful and emotional in response to her son's comments and blamed her husband for constantly raising his voice.

Tom was aware that his own response to Jake was unnecessarily forceful. He decided that something needed to be done to mend the rifts that were developing at a time when his son most needed their parental support and guidance. He agreed with Lisa that he would have a one-to-one chat with Jake and suggested to his son that they should find a convenient time later that day to talk. Tom was calm, reasonable and respectful of his son's other commitments, but was firm in his insistence that they spoke that day. Jake was grudging in his appreciation of the suggestion, but agreed that they needed to talk. Tom's open approach gave his son the opportunity to take stock before they spoke, which put the conversation on an even footing and allowed both sides to have their say.

The outcome was that Jake was able to explain to Tom that he felt his mother was disappointed in him and disliked his friends, and that made him act in a defensive way. He agreed that Lisa deserved his respect and had a right to know when he was coming home and whether other people were coming to the house

– but he felt unable to talk to her, and felt guilty when she became
upset. It was their first step towards honest communication.
Tom was able to offer some reassurance and perspective on the
situation and warmly welcomed Jake's suggestion that he should
have a similar chat with Lisa.

Guidelines for discussion:

○ Choose an appropriate time and place to talk.

○ State the problem directly:

'I am concerned that we have not been getting along recently
and that you don't seem able to...'

○ Highlight the consequences if the situation should
continue.

○ Criticize the outcomes, not the person:

'Your late-night guitar playing is disturbing the neighbours';
rather than, 'You're inconsiderate.'

○ Ask for a response.

○ Listen consciously.

○ Work out a solution together.

○ Gain commitment to action.

○ Set a deadline for review.

These guidelines are relevant in any situation where
disagreement and conflict need to be managed with a
calm, clear head. The more we can encourage our children
to think assertively and confidently, the happier adults
they will be.

Social confidence

It is in social situations that many people feel the least confident. The traits described on pp. 104-5 can be felt acutely when meeting new people, or in situations where you're unsure of what to expect or feel uncomfortable.

Take a reality check, and a self-talk check. Make sure your personal signals are as positive as possible. If the associations are negative, your belief in your ability to get your point across will drop immediately. If, on the other hand, you choose to think of every challenge in a positive light and with a sense of belief in your ability, your brain will trigger positive associations and put you in a frame of mind to succeed. To remind yourself of how this works, revisit Chapter 2. In sport, a positive attitude may mean the difference between winning and losing. Socially, the same is true.

To some extent you can plan ahead with what you are going to say socially, too – but the danger is that you will sound stilted and awkward if beset by shyness. A simpler and more spontaneous method is to revisit the question styles on p. 90; practise using them and find ways to focus more on others than you do on yourself when you go out. The guidelines aren't just for evenings out – they count in shops, pubs, at work and on other occasions, too.

The following chapter talks more about this and shows how vital body language is to being noticed and making your mark.

Release your potential – step 4: Act positive

The value of planning, listening and positive feedback

Feelings of discomfort about speaking in public will make you focus inwards instead of outwards. The more aware you are of yourself, the less you will be aware of other people, and the greater your tendency towards embarrassment, blushing, nervous tension and fears of all kinds. The way around this is to focus on others instead of yourself – but to be well prepared:

○ Plan ahead to decide not just what you want to say, but what others may say as well, so that you are fully prepared.

○ Focus on other people rather than yourself – and keep asking questions.

○ Listen well and stay focused – it will help keep the conversation on track.

Dealing with people you find difficult can be daunting – until you remember that they are people too. In order for them to see life from your perspective, you need to demonstrate that you can see life from theirs as well. If you know that the conversation is going to be a difficult one, it is invaluable to write down:

○ Your feelings – so that they do not take you by surprise while you are talking.

○ What you want to say – so that you are prepared and can express yourself clearly.

○ Solutions – suggestions of what will resolve the situation.

○ Consequences – if the situation is not resolved.

After the event, ask yourself:

❍ What was the problem?

❍ Who was involved?

❍ What actually happened?

❍ What did you want to happen?

By getting used to monitoring your reactions and responses you will gain knowledge of your personal style, as well as feel confident about the outcome of a situation.

Managing confrontation

The guidelines for managing confrontation are simple to read, but will take practice to implement.

❍ Choose your moment.

❍ Criticize the behaviour, not the person.

❍ Explain how the behaviour made you feel.

❍ Be specific.

❍ Explain the consequences.

⑤ Looking the part
How to speak body language

'You gain strength and courage and confidence by every experience in which you really stop to look fear in the face.'

ELEANOR ROOSEVELT

How confident is your body language?

Body language is instinctive and it reflects the way we are feeling inside. Are you portraying outwardly the level of confidence that you feel inwardly? If you are thinking and acting in a positive manner it will show in your bearing and the enthusiasm and life in your voice. If, on the other hand, there are seeds of doubt, or you feel shy or uncomfortable about speaking up, your feelings will show in your posture, your expressions and your gestures.

We all judge people, especially when we meet them for the first time. We read their body language intuitively. The majority of people will form a fairly strong opinion within minutes of meeting someone new and that gut reaction is likely to remain until they get to know them in more depth and re-programme their original thoughts. Voice, posture and facial expressions combine to send clear messages to others as to how we feel about ourselves, about those around us, and about our own situation.

Our initial impressions are formed, not so much by how someone looks or dresses (although that does affect the impact of that first meeting), but more by reading posture, assessing tone of voice, noting eye contact, watching for communication signals and signs of personal mood, and getting a sense of personal energy and passion. These unconscious signals can be hard to feign – certainly for any length of time – because they are an outward expression of an inner state of mind.

Of course, we also read the more superficial messages that are relayed through conscious choices, such as hairstyle, choice of clothes, the state of someone's shoes, their nails, skin and their attractiveness. These are conscious signals that say more about how someone wants to project him- or herself. These are the signals that are under our direct control.

Whether the signals are conscious or unconscious, body language speaks volumes about personality, character, self-image and levels of confidence.

When we're under pressure to perform, either socially or at work, our body language can signal our inner tension. Hunched shoulders, shallow breathing, nervous speech – all these factors can undermine the most careful preparation and will also convey our uncertainty and lack of confidence to those with whom we are talking.

We can't see our own faces, so we become reliant on interpreting other people's responses to our words and facial expressions in order to establish how we are coming across to them. The previous chapters considered how you can think and talk your way to confident behaviour, whereas this chapter takes a more physical approach. Here we take a closer look at the different styles of body language: suggesting ways to become more body confident, more observant of the signals that other people are giving out, and to make sure that your body language is not undermining the message that you want to put across.

Actions speak louder than words

Our body language is generally very honest and gives things away that we may not be conscious of ourselves. Experts in the field talk about micro-gestures, such as an inadvertent twitch or eyebrow movement, which can relay information (especially to those we know well), so that others can detect immediately if we are lying or feeling uncomfortable. Certain gestures are universal. For example, an upright posture and a warm smile are generally recognized as showing confidence or happiness, whereas slumped shoulders and a frown will convey sadness or tension, no matter how loudly you use words to suggest the contrary.

It is possible for an enthusiastic amateur to hold the attention of a group of people and to motivate them into action simply because their voice and gestures are alive with energy. Likewise, there are managers who are very knowledgeable and experienced, who lose the interest of their team because their wavering self-confidence reveals itself via non-verbal messages.

Think of your facial expressions and your body as communication tools. As with any tools, it can be useful to learn how to use them to greater effect. This does not mean acting in a way that is artificial or alien to you – but instead becoming aware enough of the kinds of messages you may be conveying that you can adapt them as necessary. It is basically a matter of unlearning the habits that are not useful to you and replacing them with ones that are more effective.

Perfecting your posture

The way you stand and move speaks volumes about how comfortable you are with life, your body and with yourself. Generally speaking, if we are feeling under threat we will tense up, triggering the 'fight or flight' response. In 'flight' mode, gestures become small, the voice may be light, breathing will be shallow, and we look physically as if we would like to escape. Conversely, at the other extreme, the 'fight' response may lead someone to dominate the situation by trying to make themselves bigger, by putting hands on hips, standing with feet apart, speaking in a loud voice, interrupting, and so on. Both these responses are likely to increase anxiety levels.

Have you ever seen someone from behind and been struck by how tired or old they look? That same person might be vibrant and confident face to face but in a relaxed and off-guard moment, their body tells a different story. We all retain tension in our bodies, but to hold on to that tension without releasing it can lead to clenched muscles, a stooping back, tensed jaw and a permanent frown. It can be difficult to shake off these habits, but they will affect the impact you have on other people. Holding a lot of such tension in your body will also make it harder to appear relaxed and confident to others.

Stand up as you are reading this paragraph, and pause for a few minutes to take stock of how you are standing.

Stand in a relaxed pose, with your feet slightly apart and your arms by your side.

Starting at the top of your body:
❍ Is your head upright and looking ahead, slightly down, or tilted slightly up?
❍ Can you feel any tension in your jaw?
❍ Can you feel any tension in your shoulders? Are they hunched up because of tension? Are they relaxed and centred, or tensed backwards?

How are you standing?
❍ Is your weight distributed evenly on both feet, or more on one side of your body than the other?
❍ Are you on the centre of your feet, leaning forwards or leaning back?

How do you move?
❍ Are you constantly rushing about, slow and sluggish, or moving smoothly and in a relaxed fashion?

How upright are you?

○ Is your pelvis tipped forward, giving you an exaggerated stomach?

○ Is it tipped back, or comfortably central?

How tense are you?

○ Are your toes and fingers clenched, or open?

Notice where the tension is in your body and take the time to consciously relax each set of muscles so that your posture becomes upright, centred and relaxed.

Relaxed posture is upright and comfortable, with weight distributed evenly across both sides of your body, and on the centre of your feet. Your pelvis will be central, your toes and fingers unclenched, and you will move at an easy, steady pace. The more often you can do this, the more naturally you will begin to improve your posture and to appear relaxed. When your muscles are relaxed you are much more likely to feel confident because the tension in your body has disappeared, literally.

The problem with feeling tense is that it can make gestures seem hostile rather than welcoming. A smile becomes a frown, a tense jaw looks threatening and hunched shoulders appear aggressive. If you don't appear relaxed, there is more scope for being misunderstood, which will undermine confidence and send the wrong message.

The following list of gestures sums up the common outward signs of confidence.

The instant confidence checklist:

Gesture	Sign of confidence
Direct gaze	Nothing to hide, confident in relationships
Smiling	Happy, confident, at ease
Head erect, good posture	High self-esteem
Open gestures	Open, honest person
Head on one side	Listening positively
Leaning forward	Engaged, listening to what is being said
Nodding	Approval of another person's point of view

If these traits are exaggerated they can come across either as being overbearing or unassertive, but an upright posture combined with these simple movements will convey balance and confidence – which will in turn prompt a positive response from others, and boost your own confidence.

Negative signals

There are several physical gestures that have come to be associated with negative or blocking styles of communication. Everyone is different; these gestures may mean a variety of things that are nothing to do with being negative, but they may nevertheless show a lack of complete confidence in a situation. The following body signals are to be avoided if you want to make a strong, confident first impression:

○ Arm crossing or folding

○ Ankle crossing

○ Holding an object (such as a file or a bag) as a physical barrier in front of you

○ Finger tapping or other physical twitching

○ Looking past someone's shoulder

○ Nose rubbing

○ Hiding your mouth

Generally speaking, the more open and relaxed your gestures, the more confident you will appear.

The eyes have it

Your facial expressions are an instant messaging system that convey how assured or not you are feeling, and your eyes are the most expressive part of your face. They are ever changing: in size, shape, depth of colour, size of pupil. The pupils of the eye dilate when you are excited by something, or in dimmed light, and contract when in bright conditions, or when in an angry or negative state. Eyes relay our emotions and our responses in an instant and are the hardest part of the face to control consciously – hence the tradition of 'looking someone in the eye' when you are talking to them.

How easy do you find it to make eye contact? Often it depends on the circumstances, but there is a tendency for people with a passive approach to find it harder to maintain eye contact than those who are more assertive.

Confident people make eye contact comfortably.

Their eyes are wide open; they are able to hold a gaze without staring, and to look around the room to take in other people without their eyes darting nervously or appearing uninterested in the person they are talking to.

Someone who is shy or less confident may find themselves looking away, or down, or even closing their eyes for a time while talking. While there is nothing wrong with this, there is scope for being misunderstood because avoiding eye contact is also associated with deception. Likewise, holding a stare too long – especially if leaning forward at the same time – can be perceived as intimidating and an invasion of personal space.

In his influential book, *Body Language*, Allan Pease recommends the following 'gazes' for different situations:

In business conversations it is important to maintain an equal relationship, and not to keep looking down in submissive manner.

The business gaze: Imagine a triangle on the forehead of the person you are talking to. The base line joins the pupils of the eyes; the peak is above the centre of the eyebrows. In order to maintain credibility and control, don't let your gaze drop below the eye level of the person you are talking to.

He also describes two other forms of gaze that denote other kinds of relationship:

The social gaze: This develops when the eyes drop down below the other person's eye level to focus on a triangular area in the centre of the face, from the pupils down to the mouth.

The intimate gaze: This extends the social gaze to take in other areas of the face and body as well.

Consider how you react in a business situation. Which area of the face do you focus on? The eyes and upwards; the eyes and the centre of the face; or the eyes and downwards? Are you inadvertently giving out social messages when you actually want to appear businesslike?

If you are unsure of the impact you are having on people you meet, ask a friend or someone close to you to help you to work on your eye contact.

Practise the business gaze, the social gaze and the intimate gaze, to become familiar with the differences between them – and to test their effect!

Work through the following list of emotions and, without speaking, use your eyes and facial expression to convey your meaning to your partner.

'I am serious about this.'
'I am passionate about the idea.'
'I am angry.'
'I would love to.'
'I am sorry.'
'It's nice to meet you.'

Try not to exaggerate your expressions. The idea is to see how effectively you can communicate – primarily with your eyes, but using the rest of your face as well. Did they get the right message?

There are no clear-cut guidelines as to how and when to use these techniques as every business and social situation is different and has to be assessed on its own merits. You are the only person who can assess the mood of your meeting and know the relationship you have with each of the people involved. However, if you are conscious of feeling nervous, or of not being taken seriously, try using the business gaze for more effective results. If, on the other hand, you feel less than confident that you are creating an impression socially, then try the social or intimate gaze to soften your impact and to make your mark in a more subtle way.

More than 80 per cent of all the information we receive is delivered to the brain via the eyes, which means that other people will form 80 per cent of their opinion based upon what they see in us. Of course, the eyes alone do not convey the message. If you want to appear approachable – smile! It will help you to feel more positive and self-confident at the same time.

Use your voice

The human voice is a vital part of communication. It's not what you say, but the way that you say it that is important. Although a letter or an email can have immense impact, words are given greater weight by the tone of your voice and your accompanying gestures.

Ask yourself:

How would you, and others, describe your voice and style of speech?

○ Are you soft-spoken or strident?

○ Do you rush your sentences or speak slowly?

○ Do you speak with a regional or other accent?

○ Do you shout to make yourself heard, or go silent?

What does your face tell people as you speak?

○ Do you smile and nod as you talk?

○ Do you frown a lot?

○ Are you impassive?

○ How often do you smile when you talk?

Making an impact means having the confidence to express yourself clearly and assertively. The key communication tools are:

○ Adjusting your tone of voice to avoid being too loud or too quiet.

○ Adjusting the speed of your speech to avoid it being too fast or too slow.

○ Avoiding long pauses or filling spaces with 'ums', 'ahs' and other nervous responses (such as giggling).

The level and tone of your voice will obviously alter depending upon whether you are speaking to someone privately, presenting to a group of people, meeting new people at a dinner, selling yourself at an interview or negotiating a business deal.

Speaking quietly, giggling and looking away from the person that you are speaking to will convey childlike behaviour that will not be taken seriously from a business or adult point of view. Likewise, a strident voice that doesn't pause to take in comments from others, and which is accompanied by aggressive gestures, will be an instant turn-off for anyone listening.

Be aware that if you have a quiet voice it may genuinely be hard for others to hear you, so you might like to practise using your voice in a more assertive manner. (If you find raising your voice a challenge, look back at the 'over the top' exercise in Chapter 3, p. 88.) Those who are naturally bullish can recognize when they are overdoing it from the way that people on the receiving end back away or avoid discussion. If this sounds like you, slow down, breathe, take pauses, and don't forget to listen to other people. Getting a positive response to what you are saying once you modify your tone is the ideal confidence boost. Soften your impact by smiling.

Ask those who know you whether they find your voice too loud or too quiet. Use relaxation and breathing techniques to help prevent constriction and shallow breathing, which will make your voice sound tense and breathless. If you practise using the upper and lower registers of your vocal range you will learn to modify your voice on demand and to project confidence – even if you are not feeling it.

Being aware of and managing the inflection in your voice is important. A harsh tone will make a simple statement sound like a criticism; a question mark at the end of a statement can undermine what you have said; and a lightness of tone when you are saying something serious will undermine the gravity of what you are saying.

Try to match the tone to the content of what you are saying. Don't worry about people's responses – you can't please everyone – but you can be true to yourself and your own feelings about what you are saying.

Myra was an account manager in her mid-30s. She was articulate, intelligent and very effective on paper, but she found difficulty in 'closing the deal' when she met with her clients face to face. As a result, meetings caused her a lot of anxiety.

Her wake-up call came in the middle of a meeting one day when her client's boss burst into the room and began to talk – completely disregarding Myra, who was writing down what was being discussed. Her client stopped the interruption and paused to introduce Myra, at which point the boss apologized profusely for interrupting with the excuse: 'I'm so sorry, I thought you were the new secretary.'

Myra realized that her anxiety was affecting her body language and she was giving out the wrong message. Far from sitting tall and leading the meeting, she was crouched and hunched, taking unnecessary notes instead of directing the conversation, and giving the impression that she was taking dictation from her client. It was time to review her body language and the impression it was creating with other people.

Mixed signals

Broadly speaking, would you label yourself as a nice person? Do you like to think that you would be able to put the needs of others before your own? While kindness and consideration are essential characteristics in life, some people take this principle to such an extreme that they find it hard to say 'no' to people at all.

If you are one of the many who can't find the right words to reject a suggestion, or you feel unable to say 'no' to an invitation, or to put your needs first, your lack of assertiveness may affect your confidence in your ability to achieve your goals. People who are nice out of habit rather than judgement are likely to give out mixed signals when they disagree with something.

Confusing characteristics:

Nodding – although you're in disagreement.
Smiling – while telling someone you are angry.
Apologizing – for something that is not your fault.
Saying 'yes' – when you want to say 'no'.
Agreeing – and then expressing an opposing view.
Voicing enthusiasm – for something that you don't support.
Dramatic gestures – that draw more attention to you than to the other person.

If you give out contradictory signals, you will cause confusion – and possibly resentment or suspicion, as people won't know where they stand. In a work situation that may mean that staff or colleagues feel free to do as they please with no fear of recrimination. At home the lack of clarity may lead to a lack of respect and a sense of not having a true voice. People who are trapped within the constraints of their 'nice' label may find themselves compromising their own intentions more often than necessary.

Look back at p. 27 at the characteristics that many people display when they are feeling unassertive, and also at p. 29 to remind yourself of your dominant reactions under pressure. Now think about events and situations that trigger such feelings.

Try to recall a situation that is relevant to you and use it as an example to help you decide how you might alter your behaviour in future in order to be more effective.

○ Describe the situation that caused you difficulty.

○ Think about your immediate reaction to the situation.

○ Did your body language or verbal signals convey a mixed message?

○ Could that have contributed to the problem?

○ How do you feel about that realization?

○ Consider what you would prefer to do differently.

○ Make a decision to practise being more assertive in future situations.

○ Draw up a plan of action to increase effectiveness.

For example, concentrate on breaking the 'apologizing habit'; re-train yourself to use open body language and more commanding gestures.

Looking confident

Your appearance offers a wealth of clues to tell the world how you really feel about yourself or the situation you are in. Are your clothes supporting your confident message, or do they undermine it? Does the state of your hair, nails or shoes show that you take care of yourself, or does it suggest self-neglect?

Uncovering your own personal style is an important element in releasing your true potential in life. Paying attention to your appearance, rather than hiding away, will feed your sense of self-worth and attractiveness, which is essential to confident communication. Using the language of clothes to bolster you in a situation where you feel nervous will help boost your confidence in your ability to achieve your goal. Equally, paying great attention to what you are going to say but neglecting your own appearance, will diminish the power of your words and leave a negative visual impression.

Take some time to review how others regard you and what positive steps you could take to make the best of yourself. No matter how strong your desire to be invisible in certain situations, you can be certain that you *will* be noticed and remembered.

Taking a risk with your appearance can jump-start a change in perspective. Many people, especially women, know that a new item of clothing or a successful haircut can boost feelings of self-confidence instantly. Using clothes as props to assist you in your transformation – such as wearing a suit in a business situation, or a flattering dress for a social occasion – can be invaluable. Ask yourself whether you are making the best of yourself or whether you are hiding behind your clothes. Does your personal style add to or detract from your current levels of confidence and self-belief?

Act the part

Confident communication shows in a dynamic combination of positive thoughts, words, actions and body language. Achieving a lasting transformation can be a slow process, but every step and every success brings positive rewards and takes you closer to realizing your full potential.

If you are feeling less than confident in your ability, you can always choose to act the part until you feel that you have genuinely made it your own. As described in Chapter 1, the mind believes what it is told and, with practice, it will replace old negative habits with positive new ones. If you begin by adopting a new stance as an experiment (envisaging yourself as someone else, if that helps), before long you will find the action comes naturally. You may want to consider a training course or working with a counsellor to help achieve this.

Trust in your own ability to transform yourself and you will become as confident as you truly want to be.

Release your potential – step 5: Look positive

Develop whole body confidence using voice, expression and posture

Body language is the clearest language of communication. It is possible to have a very honest or intimate conversation using only eyes and gestures, with no use of speech at all.

Actions speak louder than words

Many of the gestures that we use in our body language are involuntary – it is the subconscious ones that give away our true state of mind. Becoming more aware of your posture and practising relaxation techniques will help you to ensure that your body language remains positive.

○ Follow the guidelines on p. 130.

The eyes have it

Your eyes are the windows to the soul – or so it is said. So it is unsurprising that our eyes give away more about us than any other part of our bodies.

For those who find it difficult to maintain confident eye contact, there is a simple technique that will encourage you to hold your gaze in the centre of the person's face that you are talking to, without staring and without dropping your eyes in an unassertive way.

○ See pp. 134–5 for how to hold the business gaze, the social gaze and the intimate gaze.

Use your voice

Your voice has an infinite variety of tone and volume of sound. By learning to use your voice effectively you can guide the mood and pace of a conversation.

○ See p. 137 for guidelines on how to assess your level and tone of voice.

Avoid mixed messages

Many people find it hard to say 'no' or to voice disapproval. As a result, they may give out a confusing array of mixed messages, whereby their voice says one thing, but their body language says another.

Confident communication means having the courage to be yourself and to speak honestly with both voice and body. With these abilities comes an immediate increase in personal confidence because you are freed up to be yourself.

See p. 140 for a list of confusing characteristics to avoid.

The keys to confident communication are:

○ Maintain good eye contact.

○ Adjust your tone of voice to avoid being too loud or too quiet.

○ Adapt the speed of your speech to avoid it being too fast or too slow.

○ Avoid long pauses or filling spaces with 'ums', 'ahs' and other nervous responses (such as giggling).

○ Focus on remaining relaxed and don't forget to breathe.

❍ Keep your body upright and composed.

❍ Make sure your movement is controlled rather than exaggerated or nervous.

❍ Avoid aggressive hand movements, such as pointing.

Keeping on track
How to overcome setbacks

*'Whether you think you can or think you can't
– you are right.'*

HENRY FORD

Everyone faces setbacks in life and there will be times when choosing to be upbeat or confident will be a personal challenge. If you find that self-doubt has got the upper hand, or that a bout of negativity is overwhelming your desire to be confident or assertive, there is always a way to get yourself back on track.

Learning new skills takes time, and practice. It is one thing to understand the reasons for your feelings or to know how you should be behaving and what changes you need to bring about; it is quite another to make those changes – and to make them permanent.

The good news is that self-questioning is a positive trait. It allows room for personal improvement and ensures that complacency doesn't get the upper hand. Without self-doubt there would be no desire to change and no progression.

In time, confident behaviour can become a way of life. In the short term, however, you may feel you are taking one step forwards and two steps back. This is not unusual when learning a new skill. Whether learning to swim, drive a car or developing a new set of skills for a job, initial enthusiasm will probably lead to a plateau in understanding at some point, as well as temporary doubts about ever being able to 'get it right'. However, with practice, nine times out of ten we *do* get it right – and in time we wonder how we ever found the task difficult. Learning to communicate and behave in a confident manner is no different.

Emergency action

You know that the key to expressing yourself confidently lies in what you think, how you speak and the way that you project yourself. But no matter how well you prepare for a situation where you need to take an assertive approach, it is likely that you will feel a sense of anxiety or nervous anticipation.

If you are suffering from last-minute nerves or tension there is little point in questioning whether you should be better prepared. As the moment approaches, all you can do is focus on thinking and looking positive.

The key to feeling and sounding confident is to look and sound relaxed, so take the following steps to calm yourself prior to a challenging moment:

❍ Stand upright, with your weight balanced evenly across the length of both feet.

❍ Check your posture. Make sure that you are not carrying any unnecessary tension in your jaw, your shoulders, your lower back, your fingers, toes or anywhere else in your body.

○ If you are frowning, make a conscious effort to smile. It will release the tension.

○ Link your fingers and stretch your arms above your head as far as they will go; move them to the front and to your sides then re-link them behind your back.

○ Yawn and take a series of deep breaths – breathing in from your diaphragm (just below the rib cage) rather than from your upper chest. This will replenish your lungs with fresh air, and help relax you and calm your nerves.

○ Shake your arms, hands and fingers, as well as your legs. It will get rid of excess tension in your body.

○ If you are feeling angry, upset or fearful, conjure up an amusing situation in your mind. It is hard to be angry or upset if you are laughing.

○ Watch your body language and keep your gestures open and your gaze at eye level.

○ Finally – remind yourself of your goal and your motivation. If you are motivated you will feel upbeat, positive and energetic. It will be much harder to let anyone else's negativity affect you if you are in a confident frame of mind.

Taking stock

If you are experiencing temporary or ongoing setbacks, ask yourself why that might be.

What's your goal?

○ Do you know what you want and what you're trying to achieve?

○ Are you striving to achieve *your* goal – or someone else's?

○ Do you know what is motivating you to achieve your goal?

○ Do you have everything you need to achieve it?

○ Or do you need to break down each stage into more manageable pieces?

The more control you have over your situation, the less anxious you will feel and the more confidence you will have in your ability to be assertive or to talk about an issue effectively. If your goal is too vague, or you are trying to achieve too many things at once, you will undermine your own success. If this is the case for you, take stock of each situation, and then decide on your list of priorities.

○ What kinds of feelings are you experiencing?

○ Are you plagued by nervousness, fear, anticipation, anger or resistance?

○ Are you feeling generally positive or negative about the situation?

○ If you are feeling negative, what do you need to do, or what needs to happen, to change that situation around?

Remember: Just because a challenge exists, it does not mean that you have to rise to it – especially if it is a situation that you fundamentally don't believe in or don't want to be associated with.

What is the problem?

○ Are the feelings you are experiencing related to having to face the situation, to the way you relate to a person involved in the situation, or to the consequences of the outcome?

○ Which aspects of the situation are within your control, and which are in the control of someone else?

○ Are you making the situation bigger than it really is?

○ Refer back to p. 71 for a reality check. Where is the evidence for your concerns? If it is real, how can you prepare to overcome those issues?

What are the solutions to the situation?

○ Is the solution to the situation totally in your hands, or do you need the expertise of others to help you to achieve your goal?

○ Is your current plan of action enough to solve the situation, or is it simply a first step?

○ Do you need to consider alternative solutions that may address the situation more completely?

What do you want to say?

○ To help prepare for the situation, write down what you want to say.

○ Practise role-playing the situation – either on your own or with the help of someone you trust to help you in a constructive manner.

○ Refer back to p. 90 for examples of the styles of question that you can use to draw out other people.

What sort of outcome do you want?

o Think about the difference in the consequences or outcomes of your situation, depending on the style of approach you choose to take.

o Which outcome would you prefer – and what do you have to do to prepare for that outcome?

o Refer back to p. 66 to ask yourself, 'What if...?' and 'So what...'. If you can look your anxiety in the face by coming to terms with every possible outcome, you will stop the problem being larger than it needs to be.

Managing your emotions

Our emotions are at the heart of our ability to act, feel or speak in a confident manner. If you believe in your ability, you will be confident; if you have doubts, it will take longer for you to achieve your aim.

As explained in Chapter 1, our emotions can be triggered in an instant. Unexpected memories or associations will take us back to previous situations where we felt unconfident or unsure of our ability to cope.

If you are fearful that you will be overwhelmed by your emotions, concentrate your attention on those around you so that you are looking outwards instead of inwards. It may also help you to create a visualization and pre-prepare an absurd solution whenever you see yourself crying or becoming angry.

For example:

If you see yourself crying and fear it, transform the situation into something comical instead. Witty remarks or humour are the ideal way to diffuse distress or anger. If you have a good imagination, transform the situation into a scene from a comedy!

If you are tempted towards anger, try to imagine something that you associate with feeling upbeat and positive, such as a small child laughing and giving you a gift, tearing along a country road on a motorbike, or playing your favourite music.

The better prepared you are to use such images, the more quickly you can nip inappropriate emotions in the bud. This is not to deny your feelings, but to help express them in way that is more constructive.

Another way to manage emotions is to pre-empt them and to write down or rehearse how you feel.

Tim was an advertising executive who worked for a high-achieving and highly demanding manager, who thought nothing of shouting at and belittling members of her team. Tim loathed conflict and attempted to avoid it at all costs. He resented his manager's attitude and was harbouring an immense amount of anger towards her. Matters came to a head when she criticized him in front of a major client.

Tim knew that he had to tackle the situation. He managed to contain himself for long enough to arrange a meeting with her the following day. Concerned that his pent-up emotions would break out in anger, he and his wife Penny role-played the discussion that he would have with her the next morning. It was a tough and very emotional rehearsal but, as a result, Tim vented his extreme emotions in the safety of his own home. He felt completely calm and prepared when he entered the office to speak to his boss the next morning and was able to focus on the core issues.

Sally was a midwife who took responsibility for bringing new life into the world almost every day of her life. She was calm, reassuring and highly professional. In her personal life, insecurity about her looks undermined her self-confidence and prevented her from making any male friends. A critical voice inside her head constantly undermined her belief that anyone would find her attractive or interesting.

Aware that she was her own worst enemy, she spent some time writing down those aspects of her character that she knew she could respect, and also thought about what she would ideally like to say to someone she wanted to get to know better. In addition, she set herself the personal goal of improving her self-image – and asked a friend to help her stretch her shopping boundaries. It took more than one attempt for Sally to turn the theory into reality, but the act of mental preparation spurred her into action – and personal transformation. Positive feedback from friends and colleagues about her new look helped to boost her confidence and belief in the possibility of acting differently, while still being herself.

The voice of disapproval can be very loud and extremely persistent in vulnerable moments. If you have prepared positive ways to counter the negatives when they rear their head, you are well on your way to making your positive communication skills permanent.

A word about self-esteem

For some people, the underlying reason for poor communication skills runs deeper than the need to learn some practical techniques and raise self-awareness. The ability to feel confident and to act in an assertive way depends on your level of self-esteem. Without self-esteem it will be hard to hold a favourable opinion of yourself, or to appreciate your unique skills and abilities.

The following behaviours could be signs that you are suffering from low self-esteem:

❍ You habitually put yourself down.

❍ You tend to avoid challenges and new opportunities.

❍ You always see the reasons why *not* to do something.

❍ You are generally reluctant to accept positions of responsibility.

❍ You often allow others to make decisions for you.

❍ You choose to spend a lot of time alone.

❍ You may be highly-strung and over analytical.

❍ You have a tendency to worry or feel depressed.

❍ You depend heavily on other people.

The reasons for low self-esteem are wide and varied, and beyond the scope of this book. The sense that you are unworthy of care and affection may be related to self-image, to a sense of loss, or to events buried in your childhood.

This book is not a substitute for professional advice or help with depression or anxiety. If you know that your personal fears and concerns run deep and are threatening your well-being, please choose to be kinder to yourself by asking for professional help. Talking to a trained counsellor or psychologist will help you to re-frame your past experiences in a supportive environment and enable you to examine the way you look at life in a constructive way.

Low self-esteem generally results in a sense of powerlessness and unworthiness, which may lead to difficulty in accepting constructive criticism or to feeling your voice is unheard in a group.

The following suggestions are good confidence boosters, whatever your level of self-esteem:

o Make sure your goals are achievable – and plan realistic steps to attain them.

o Stop self-criticism and concentrate on your positive qualities.

o Focus on your achievements and the times when you felt good about yourself.

o Practise positive affirmations that will develop your self-belief.

o Make time to relax and unwind – it will help to put life in perspective.

o Accept that you have limitations.

o Don't commit to doing more than you can realistically achieve.

o If you are given a compliment – accept it with good heart.

o Try not to think in extremes. Reality is never as simple as black and white.

o Choose your friends and contacts wisely. Make sure they support and do not undermine you.

❍ Take things one step at a time and be patient. Permanent change happens slowly and steadily.

Overcoming low self-esteem is not a simple matter of 'snapping yourself out of it'. First you need to see that no matter what the situation is, you *do* have personal choice – even if it is to do with choosing your attitude. Once you understand that it is you, not other people, who is in control of who you are and what you think, it becomes possible to transform low self-esteem into self-confidence.

Which track is the right track?

Other setbacks can be the result of trying to achieve or make a success of something that is contrary to your nature. If you are trying to be someone you are not, or are holding back from being all you could be to spare someone else's feelings, it will impact on your ability to communicate positively.

Make a list of the values and aspirations that you consider to be important and select the six that are closest to the way you try to live your life. Now ask yourself: are they in tune with your choice of career or relationship?

For example:

If your main drivers are making a difference, positive relationships and helping others, you may find great satisfaction working in the caring professions, whereas a purely commercial environment may not fulfil all your ambitions. A large distance between personal need and your role in real life can undermine your ability to perform or communicate confidently.

You may be a high achiever who is motivated towards further success by material goals. Being true to who you are is an important part of self-confidence. Compromising personal goals or ideals leads to confusion about where we are headed. Ambition is an important driver in the development of confidence. If you believe in your goal, it will be eaier to take a few knocks and to communicate your intentions strongly.

Assessing which of the following aspects are the most important to you will help you to understand what motivates you in life and what will affect your choice of work, as well as influence your relationships.

Material rewards
Personal influence
Having expertise
Search for meaning
Creativity
Relationships
Independence
Security
Status

Be honest with yourself when determining what really drives you – recognizing your personal strengths and being true to your own nature will help you to express yourself and communicate more comfortably.

Don't rush

When under pressure it is easy to rush, or to try to respond to a pace being set by others. Keeping on track means being conscious enough of what you are saying and what you are doing to stay in control of the situation. Concern about what to say or what has been said can inhibit the ability to fully participate in a meeting or conversation. If you make a mistake or feel that you shouldn't have said something, don't dwell on it. Take a deep breath, and keep going – at a calm pace.

If you can hear yourself speeding up when speaking, or are aware that you are sounding breathless, subtly take a deep breath and slow down. After each question, leave time for reply – don't feel that you have to leap in to fill the silence.

Watch your tone of voice and don't be dismissive of what you are saying. If you want other people to take you seriously, you need to take yourself seriously – and demonstrate your belief in what you have to say.

Remember your friends and family

Keeping on track with friends and family is essential to positive and healthy relationships. It is easy to assume that because we are related to someone, or live with them, that they will instinctively know and understand what we mean.

Communication problems at home can often be resolved quite easily with some honest discussion. Take it in turns to say what is on your mind. Comment on the actions and your feelings, not the person. Other people can only tell what you want and how you feel if you tell them.

The future

The future will arrive whether or not we feel confident, but one thing is certain – staying focused and working to maintain self-belief will inevitably lead to an increase in confidence. You will feel much more in control and will experience more enjoyment of life in the future.

Release your potential – step 6: Live positive

Take stock, refocus, be yourself

Setbacks are a normal part of life and it is how we deal with them, rather than the challenge itself, that is important. There is always something you can do to get yourself back on track, and new skills require practice before they become a permanent way of life.

In the short term:

If there is no more time for preparation, you need to make the most of the moment and to make sure that your mind and body are conveying a positive message:

○ Think positive.
○ Check your posture.
○ Relax.
○ Smile.
○ Stretch.
○ Shake.
○ Laugh.
○ Be open and direct.
○ Stay focused.

In the longer term:

In the mid- to long term there is time to look more closely at the underlying reason for your anxiety. Take longer to plan and prepare:

○ Understand your feelings.
○ Be clear about your goal.

○ Have you got all the facts?
○ Think outside the box.
○ What do you want to say?
○ What do you want to happen?
○ What do you need to do?

If you understand the triggers that undermine your confidence then you will be better placed to overcome them and replace them with confidence-building techniques.

The ability to manage or channel your emotions is at the heart of feeling confident and being confident.
○ Use visualization or positive association.
○ Write out your reactions.
○ Role-play your responses.

Every time you turn negative feelings into positive, you boost your ability to communicate confidently. You also create positive memories and associations that will make the process easier in the future.

Watch your self-esteem

Confident communication is about more than learning a few techniques – it starts from within. If your lack of confidence runs deep, then you may have problems with low self-esteem. If you are having difficulty overcoming these on your own then consider getting some help, as the issues will affect your whole life.
○ Make sure your goals are achievable.

○ Be realistic.
○ Accept yourself as you are.
○ Be true to yourself.
○ Have self-belief.
○ Take your time.

No matter how far off track you have wandered, never forget your friends and family, as we all need support in difficult times.

The future will arrive whether or not you feel confident – but if you keep practising these techniques you will find yourself becoming more confident all the time and better able to face the future and all it brings.

7 Conclusion

'Change your thoughts and you change your world.'

NORMAN VINCENT PEALE

Communication starts with a thought and ends with an action or reaction. It consists of a constant to-ing and fro-ing of ideas, interpretations and impressions, which we analyze, dissect and measure against our own opinions in milliseconds, before we decide how we feel about what has been said or done and choose our next response.

Communication should be a dynamic process where new input and ideas are welcome – because it is only by sharing ideas that we can form new opinions and make things happen. Why is it then that so often we find speaking up a difficult experience?

Communication becomes difficult when people stop listening or become preoccupied solely with their own point of view or agenda, or when fear of conflict, disagreement or loss of control come into the frame. If you could be certain that when you opened your mouth you would be listened to and not judged, there would be no need to be anxious about voicing your opinions and ideas.

At the heart of most people's qualms about speaking up or not being heard is anxiety on some level of being judged unfavourably: of not being good enough, of holding an unorthodox opinion, of not fitting the status quo, and so on. If, however, you can think yourself into a frame of mind where you trust yourself and have confidence in your opinions and your ideas, the fact that other people hold different views will cease to be such a problem. The trick is to understand that, although they hold a different view, they are not dismissing you as a person in the process.

With that in mind it is important to remember to treat other people's views and opinions with respect too. Imagine how easy life would be if we could all count on being listened to and given the space to have our say – without fear of negative repercussions?

Out of difference comes originality. No one who has made a difference in the world has done it by following the crowd. The more willing you are to take a communication risk, the more likely you are to make things happen. The more often you make things happen, via your own efforts, the greater will be your belief in your ability to communicate positively and confidently.

Much of this book has been concerned with exercises designed to help you to develop practical communication skills. They are the tools that will provide the means by which you can act more assertively. At the heart of the matter is your self-belief, and your understanding that you have a right to hold your views – not at the expense of other people, but even though they may differ from those of people whose opinions you respect.

How you think and what you say to yourself remains the single most important step in learning to 'say it with confidence'. If you can turn positive thinking and self-respect for your views and opinions into a habit for life, the rest of the techniques outlined here will fall into place with ease. Thinking your own thoughts and forming your own opinions means that you are taking responsibility for your life and your actions. Turning those into measurable goals means that you will have an even deeper knowledge of who you are and what you want to achieve – and it will be easier to find your voice when you need to speak.

Communicating with confidence allows you the possibility of living your life to the full, on equal terms with others in your life, and free of any inhibitions that prevent you from being the best you can be.

Release your potential – step 7: Be confident

Think confidently, live confidently and you will communicate confidently

You owe it to yourself to be as confident as you can be so that you can become the best you are capable of being. There are great benefits to living life in a consciously confident way.

○ Live your own life – and take responsibility for it.

○ Acknowledge your own feelings – and be honest about them.

○ Communicate with respect – and respect the views of others.

○ Criticize the behaviour – not the person.

○ Recognize that passive and aggressive behaviours stem from a lack of assertiveness and a fear of being misunderstood or overlooked.

○ Always listen to the other person and respect their rights as much as your own.

○ If you feel angry or upset, learn to take time out to calm down, rather than have emotionally-charged conflicts.

○ Be patient with yourself – permanent transformation takes time.

○ Use body language in a positive way that backs up rather than contradicts what you are saying.

Seven steps to saying it with confidence

KNOW YOURSELF ➤ **THINK POSITIVE** ➤ **TALK POSITIVE** ➤ **ACT POSITIVE** ➤ **LOOK POSITIVE** ➤ **LIVE POSITIVE** ➤ **BE CONFIDENT**

Step 1: Know yourself
Appreciate your strengths, know your weaknesses and accept who you are

Reconciling yourself to who you are is an important step towards getting to the root of the matter that will help you to understand your actions and reactions.

○ Draw yourself as you see yourself. It will tell you a lot about who you are.

○ Look at your labels. Not the ones on your clothes (although they too tell a story), but the labels that you give yourself – those that either limit you or give you confidence. Make a conscious commitment to exchange negative labels for positive ones.

○ Review your core values, as they are an important part of who you are. Is there a difference between what you believe and what you say? Are you limiting yourself by staying within a comfort zone of experiences?

Keeping a journal can be a valuable way to chart your progress and to capture your thoughts and feelings as you increase in confidence and experience ups and downs.

Step 2: Think positive
Take responsibility for your thoughts and you will direct your own actions

Our thoughts become our words and our words become our actions, so it is important to think and talk to ourselves in as positive a way as possible.

Memories are powerful thoughts. A situation or conversation can trigger an unexpected or subconscious memory that results in an instant response – either positive or negative – that may not be relevant to the reality of the present moment.

Worrying about the consequences can prevent us from taking the first step towards confident action.

○ Taking a reality check (see p. 71) will help you to sort which of your views of yourself are true and which need to be viewed in perspective.

○ Use the 'What if…?' test (see p. 66) to find out what is at the root of your lack of confidence and what will help you to take action to become more assertive.

○ Take steps to turn false thinking into new and positive action. (See p. 56.)

You are the only person who can take responsibility for your thoughts, your views and your actions.

Step 3: Talk positive
Say what you mean, mean what you say and choose to say it

If you are not being heard there may be a reason. Being yourself is the key to 'saying it right' and saying it with confidence in all situations. At the root of this is the need to know your own mind and plan what you're going to say.

❍ Don't *wait* for the 'right' moment; *create* the 'right' moment.

❍ Use the four steps to assertive behaviour:

- Understand the other person.
- Express your feelings.
- Propose solutions.
- Seek feedback.

❍ Push yourself to find your voice (see p. 87).

❍ Use open, probing and closed questions to drive, rather than react to, conversations.

The art of asking questions is at the heart of speaking with confidence. To listen and also to be heard are the keys to assertive communication.

Step 4: Act positive
The value of planning, listening and positive feedback

Feelings of nervousness and discomfort will make you focus inwards instead of outwards, and you will show more embarrassment, nervous tension and fears of all kinds. The way around this is to focus on others instead of on yourself, and to be well prepared:

○ Plan ahead to decide not just what you want to say, but what others may say as well.

○ Focus on other people rather than on yourself – and keep asking questions.

○ Listen carefully and stay focused – it will help to keep the conversation on track.

Dealing with people you find difficult can be daunting – but it can help to remember that they have a right to their view too. If you know that a conversation is going to be a difficult one, it is invaluable to write down in advance:

○ Your feelings – so that they do not take you by surprise while you are talking.

○ What you want to say – so that you are prepared and can express yourself clearly.

○ Solutions – that will resolve the situation.

○ Consequences – if the situation is not resolved.

After the event, make a note of:

○ What the problem was

○ Who was involved

○ What actually happened

○ What you wanted to happen

By getting used to monitoring your reactions and responses you will gain knowledge of your personal style as well as feeling confident about the outcomes.

Managing confrontation

The guidelines for managing confrontation are simple to read, but they will take practice to implement effectively.

○ Choose your moment.

○ Criticize the behaviour, not the person.

○ Explain how the behaviour made you feel.

○ Be specific.

○ Explain the consequences.

Step 5: Look positive
Develop whole body confidence using voice, expression and posture

Body language is the clearest language of communication. Our actions speak louder than our words, but sometimes we give out mixed messages:

❍ Many of the gestures we use in our body language are involuntary. It is the subconscious gestures that give away our true state of mind.

❍ Don't let your eyes give you away. See p. 133 for guidelines on how to give the right message at the right time.

❍ Use your tone of voice to guide the mood and pace of a conversation.

❍ Measure your pace, and adjust your speed of speech to avoid it being too fast or slow.

❍ Relax and breathe.

❍ Use open gestures.

❍ Control your gestures and calm your nerves.

Step 6: Live positive
Take stock, refocus, be yourself, stay on track

Setbacks are a normal part of life and it is how we deal with them, rather than the challenge itself, that is important. Thinking positive and building your self-belief are the keys to long-term success. There is always something you can do to get yourself back on track, and new skills require practice before they become a permanent way of life.

Make sure that your mind and body are conveying a positive message:

○ Think positive.
○ Check your posture.
○ Relax and smile.
○ Stretch body and mind.
○ Be open and direct.
○ Stay focused.

Take more time to plan and prepare:

○ Understand your feelings.
○ Be clear about your goal.
○ Have you got all the facts?
○ Think outside the box.
○ What do you want to say?
○ What do you want to happen?
○ What do you need to do?

If you understand the triggers that undermine your confidence, you will be better placed to overcome them and to replace them with confidence-building techniques.

Watch your self-esteem. Confident communication is about more than learning a few techniques – it starts from within.

❍ Make sure your goals are achievable.

❍ Be realistic.

❍ Accept yourself as you are.

❍ Be true to yourself.

❍ Have self-belief.

❍ Take your time.

The future will arrive whether or not you feel confident – but if you keep practising these techniques you will find yourself becoming more confident all the time and better able to face the future and all it brings.

Step 7: Be confident
Think confidently, live confidently and you will communicate confidently

You owe it to yourself to be as confident as you can be so that you can become the best you are capable of being. There are great benefits to living life in a consciously confident way.

○ Live your own life – and take responsibility for it.

○ Acknowledge your own feelings and be honest about them.

○ Communicate with respect – and respect the views of others.

○ Be patient with yourself – permanent transformation takes time.

Further resources

Where to go for help and who does what

The information that follows will provide basic details about the main sources of help and treatment for confidence building and assertiveness. For advice on how to find and select a qualified practitioner, please contact the regulatory bodies or associations listed on these pages.

The BBC website is also an excellent source of information. Visit www.bbc.co.uk/health/confidence.

Cognitive behaviour therapy (CBT)

Cognitive behaviour therapy focuses on the connection between what you think about yourself or a situation and how you choose to react to it. CBT takes a 'here and now' approach that focuses on causes and effects in the present day, rather than delving into your past.

The aim of CBT is to break cycles of negative thinking and behaviour, and to help you to cope more effectively with life by improving your self-esteem and self-image. Research has found it to be helpful for a range of problems including low self-esteem, anxiety and the effects of stress.

The CBT approach is action-orientated. With your therapist, you will draw up time-bound and specific goals that you would like to achieve – together with the strategies you need to put in place to achieve those goals.

CBT is used by specially trained and qualified professionals, such as clinical psychologists, psychiatrists and counsellors. Your GP or a mental health professional may be able to refer you to an appropriate therapist.

If you choose to consult a cognitive behaviour therapist privately you can find a qualified professional or check their qualifications via the British Association for Behavioural and Cognitive Psychotherapies (BABCP).

British Association for Behavioural and Cognitive Psychotherapies (BABCP)

The Globe Centre
PO Box 9
Accrington
BB5 0XB
Tel: (01254) 875277
www.babcp.org.uk

Coaching

A coach is a facilitator, listener and motivator, whose role is to help the client to decide on their aims and ambitions, put in place achievable goals, and provide ongoing support to encourage the development of personal skills and self-belief to achieve those goals. Coaching differs from counselling and psychotherapy in that the relationship is driven by the client and focuses on practical outcomes, rather than addressing any deep-seated issues relating to depression, low self-esteem or poor motivation.

A coach is unlikely to share the same professional background as their client, but will use observation and questioning techniques to help the client develop their own solutions. Coaches are committed to remaining supportive and non-judgemental at all times.

Coaches will recognize when a client would be better supported by counselling and psychotherapy and may recommend an appropriate therapist if the counselling/therapy boundary is crossed.

Coaching may be the ideal solution if you need help in refocusing your goals and ambitions and have problems with prioritizing and personal motivation. Further information about the coaching process, and how it differs from mentoring, counselling and psychotherapy, can be found on the Coaching and Mentoring Network website (see below).

The Association for Coaching

66 Church Road
London
W7 1LB
www.associationforcoaching.com

The Coaching and Mentoring Network

PO Box 5551
Newbury
Berks
RG20 7WB
www.coachingnetwork.org.uk
Tel: 0870 733 3313

Counselling

Counselling involves talking one-to-one, and in complete confidence, with a trained professional, who will give you their full attention and commitment to help you to transform your stressful situation into something more positive. For those who are at a personal crossroads, working with a counsellor can be invaluable, whether problems relate to everyday concerns or deeper, long-term issues. Counselling should be a personal and voluntary decision that is never forced. To be effective it requires the complete commitment and involvement of the client as well as the counsellor. A session with a counsellor is private and everything that is discussed is treated in complete confidence.

The counsellor aims to understand difficulties from the point of view of the client by using active listening techniques, enabling the client to understand the problem from a different perspective. A sense of trust between client and counsellor is vital in order for the client to feel able to express feelings such as anger, anxiety or grief, and to get past any sense of embarrassment about showing their emotions.

The counselling process will vary according to the counsellor's training and personal approach, as well as the client's requirements and the problem itself.

There are various types of counselling including:

- ○ Cognitive behaviour therapy (CBT) - see above
- ○ Relationship counselling
- ○ Counselling based on your personal faith

○ Co-counselling – based on a system of mutual support

○ Addiction counselling – for specific substance addiction

It is vital for the relationship between client and counsellor to be both constructive and positive. If you feel uncomfortable or feel the relationship is not working, speak first to your counsellor about your concerns, but feel free to find an alternative therapist if necessary.

The British Association for Counselling and Psychotherapy can advise on how to select a qualified counsellor near you.

British Association for Counselling and Psychotherapy (BACP)

BACP House

35–37 Albert Street

Rugby

Warks

CV21 2SG

Tel: 0870 443 5252

www.bacp.co.uk

British Association of Anger Management

Tel: 0845 130 0286

www.angermanage.co.uk

Relate

Herbert Gray College

Little Church Street

Rugby
CV21 3AP
Tel: 0845 456 1310
www.relate.org.uk

Medical advice

If you suffer physical symptoms associated with your confidence issues, your GP or health centre will be a very good source of support and initial advice. Your doctor may check your blood pressure and your cholesterol levels and make general recommendations concerning diet, exercise and lifestyle. It may also be possible to be referred for counselling via the NHS, or to get other specialized help. Prescribed medicines may also be recommended as either a short-term or long-term solution, depending on the severity of the symptoms.

For those who are reluctant to consult their GP in the first instance, NHS Direct is an excellent source of information and advice.

NHS Direct

Tel: 0845 4647
www.nhsdirect.org.uk

Mentoring

Mentoring is similar in approach to coaching (see above), but a mentor is likely to be from the same professional background as their client and may well be working on a voluntary basis within an organization. A mentor's aim is to support their client and to help them to achieve their full potential by enabling them to set and achieve appropriate goals, and offering the benefit of their own experience – thereby fast-tracking the learning experience.

Whereas coaching and mentoring used to be available only for senior members of staff, it is now being used increasingly in corporations that are going through periods of extensive change as a way of boosting morale, sharing business skills and helping the organization to achieve its objectives.

If your confidence issues are related to work, the mentoring approach may well be the most appropriate solution as it takes place in the environment that is causing the problems and can therefore tackle them at source.

If you have deeper issues relating to low self-esteem, it could be valuable to seek counselling support as well. The Coaching and Mentoring Network can provide further information (see above for contact details).

Neuro-Linguistic Programming (NLP)

NLP has its roots in psychology and neurology. It is concerned with how the brain works, the different ways we each process information, and how the brain can be trained to improve learning ability and positive well-being. NLP is used as an effective way of changing negative thought processes into positive ones, and can be used as a valuable technique to improve communication skills in the workplace and socially.

It is important to check the qualifications of your NLP

trainer and to ask them to explain how they will be using the technique in order to be clear about your needs and the personal benefits you can expect. NLP is used increasingly in partnership with hypnotherapy. The Association for NLP International (ANLP) provides further information and advice on where to find a practitioner.

Association for Neuro-Linguistic Programming (ANLP)

PO Box 3357
Unit 14
Barnet
EN5 9AJ
Tel: 0870 444 0790
www.anlp.org

Psychotherapy

There are many different types of psychotherapy, all of which have been developed to help people overcome stress, emotional or relationship problems and other mental health issues. All are 'talking treatments', but, unlike psychiatry, do not rely upon medication as part of the treatment.

Psychodynamic psychotherapy focuses on past experiences and how these impact on feelings we have about other people. If problems are long-standing, treatment may take many months.

Behavioural psychotherapy focuses more directly on changing patterns of behaviour. It includes aversion therapy and desensitization techniques, which involve spending time doing or being with those things that cause anxiety. It is especially effective for anxiety-related conditions and phobias – and results can be immediate.

Family and Marital Therapy focuses on relationship problems by looking at the separate relationships between each of the people involved.

See also *Cognitive Behaviour Therapy (CBT)*, above.

A combination of these techniques may be used to suit the individual.

In individual psychotherapy, client and therapist talk one to one for 40 minutes to an hour. In group therapy, several people with similar problems will meet with a therapist or therapists. The impact of discovering you are not alone with your problem can be powerful – especially if you find you can help others overcome an aspect of their difficulties as well.

A psychotherapist may be a psychiatrist, psychologist or other mental health professional, who has had further specialist training in psychotherapy. Your GP will be able to refer you to a qualified psychotherapist in your area. It is important that a psychotherapist has a recognized qualification and you should not be afraid to choose not to work with someone with whom you do not feel comfortable.

See your GP or consult the British Association for Counselling and Psychotherapy for further information (see above for contact details).

Bibliography

BBC Learning, *Say The Right Thing: Training Guide*, BBC Worldwide Ltd (London), 2002; written to accompany *Say The Right Thing*, a two-part business learning package, BBC Worldwide Ltd (London), 2002.

Branden, Nathaniel, *The Six Pillars of Self-esteem*, Bantam (New York), 1994.

Buzan, Tony, *Embracing Change*, BBC Worldwide Ltd (London), 2005.

Buzan, Tony, *Use Your Head*, BBC Worldwide Ltd (London), 1974.

Dickson, Anne, *A Woman in Your Own Right: Assertiveness and You*, Quartet Books (London), 1982.

Golman, Daniel, *Emotional Intelligence*, Bloomsbury (London), 1996.

Jeffers, Susan, *Feel the Fear and Do It Anyway*, Arrow (London), 1991.

Lindenfield, Gael, *Managing Anger*, Thorsons (London), 2000.

Litvinoff, Sarah, *The Confidence Plan: Essential steps to a new you*, BBC Books (London), 2004.

McKenna, Paul, *Instant Confidence*, Bantam Press (London), 2006.

Morris, Desmond, *People Watching: The Desmond Morris Guide to Body Language*, Vintage (London), 2002.

Pease, Allan, *Body Language: How to Read Others' Thoughts by their Gestures*, Sheldon Press (London), 1984.

Smith, Manuel J, *When I Say No I Feel Guilty*, Bantam (London), 1981.

Taylor, Ros, *Confidence Zone: Support Notes*, BBC Learning (London), 2004; written to accompany *Confidence Zone*, a six-part business learning package, BBC Worldwide Ltd (London), 2004.

Taylor, Ros, *Transform Yourself*, Kogan Page (London), 2000.

Index